Mustang Sally

by Linda Felton Steinbaum

FOUNDED 1830

New York Hollywood London Toronto

SAMUELFRENCH.COM

Copyright © 2007, 2008 by Linda Felton Steinbaum

ALL RIGHTS RESERVED

CAUTION: Professionals and amateurs are hereby warned that *MUSTANG SALLY* is subject to a royalty. It is fully protected under the copyright laws of the United States of America, the British Commonwealth, including Canada, and all other countries of the Copyright Union. All rights, including professional, amateur, motion picture, recitation, lecturing, public reading, radio broadcasting, television and the rights of translation into foreign languages are strictly reserved. In its present form the play is dedicated to the reading public only.

The amateur live stage performance rights to *MUSTANG SALLY* are controlled exclusively by Samuel French, Inc., and royalty arrangements and licenses must be secured well in advance of presentation. PLEASE NOTE that amateur royalty fees are set upon application in accordance with your producing circumstances. When applying for a royalty quotation and license please give us the number of performances intended, dates of production, your seating capacity and admission fee. Royalties are payable one week before the opening performance of the play to Samuel French, Inc., at 45 W. 25th Street, New York, NY 10010.

Royalty of the required amount must be paid whether the play is presented for charity or gain and whether or not admission is charged.

Stock royalty quoted upon application to Samuel French, Inc.

For all other rights than those stipulated above, apply to Samuel French, Inc., at 45 W. 25th Street, New York, NY 10010.

Particular emphasis is laid on the question of amateur or professional readings, permission and terms for which must be secured in writing from Samuel French, Inc.

Copying from this book in whole or in part is strictly forbidden by law, and the right of performance is not transferable.

Whenever the play is produced the following notice must appear on all programs, printing and advertising for the play: "Produced by special arrangement with Samuel French, Inc."

Due authorship credit must be given on all programs, printing and advertising for the play.

ISBN 978-0-573-66048-1   Printed in U.S.A.   #15756

No one shall commit or authorize any act or omission by which the copyright of, or the right to copyright, this play may be impaired.

No one shall make any changes in this play for the purpose of production.

Publication of this play does not imply availability for performance. Both amateurs and professionals considering a production are strongly advised in their own interests to apply to Samuel French, Inc., for written permission before starting rehearsals, advertising, or booking a theatre.

No part of this book may be reproduced, stored in a retrieval system, or transmitted in any form, by any means, now known or yet to be invented, including mechanical, electronic, photocopying, recording, videotaping, or otherwise, without the prior written permission of the publisher.

IMPORTANT BILLING AND CREDIT REQUIREMENTS

All producers of *MUSTANG SALLY must* give credit to the Author of the Play in all programs distributed in connection with performances of the Play, and in all instances in which the title of the Play appears for the purposes of advertising, publicizing or otherwise exploiting the Play and /or a production. The name of the Author *must* appear on a separate line on which no other name appears, immediately following the title and *must* appear in size of type not less than fifty percent of the size of the title type.

MUSTANG SALLY was first presented on October 13, 2007, by Tish Smiley and Rebekah Score at the Whitefire Theatre, Sherman Oaks, California, with the following cast:

Kathy (Kitty) Van Pelt	Sally Conway
Elizabeth (Biz) Van Pelt	Andrea Conte
Tony Knight	Sean Vincent Biggins
Edward Green	Michael Blain-Rozgay
Marilyn Van Pelt	Tish Smiley

Directed by:	Arturo Castillo
Set by:	Chris Winfield
Lighting/sound by:	Eric Snodgrass
Costumes by:	Tina Rose
Stage Manager:	Vincent Archer
House Manager:	Edgar Mastin

CHARACTERS

KATHY– A nice looking, gentle 31-year-old never married, middle school music teacher. Quiet and introverted, she has always lacked confidence and social skills.

ELIZABETH – Kathy's attractive and sexy 35-year-old single sister. She was self-made and is now a sophisticated, successful businesswoman who owns four popular dance and fitness studios.

EDWARD– A divorced 45-year-old conservative, attractive lawyer. He is definitely more comfortable negotiating in the courtroom than negotiating his personal life as many long hours were spent climbing to the top.

MARILYN – Elizabeth and Kathy's 65-year-old eccentric divorced mother. A strong willed, religious zealot who dresses inappropriately youthful and garish, she worked very hard all her life and hopes to be rewarded.

TONY – A hip and friendly 25-year-old man who teaches art at Kathy's school. He is cute, artistic and a bit offbeat.

THE SCENE
The time is present. The action takes place in Kathy's modest, yet colorful apartment, Any City, USA.

ACT ONE
Late afternoon.

ACT TWO
Scene One: The next day.
Scene Two: Later that night.
Scene Three: The following afternoon.

Thanks to my champions, Bruce, Carly and Glenn for your support and our happy life together.

ACT 1

SETTING: *the time is present. All action takes place in the kitchen/den area of a simple apartment. There is a counter and a table with two chairs in the kitchen area, one chair filled with magazines. A small sofa and end tables are on the other side of the room. Flower and music oriented prints adorn the walls, a small mirror hangs near a plant stand, and a large wall calendar dangles on a nail in the kitchen. A cell phone and magazines are on the end tables. More magazines are in a magazine rack near the kitchen.*

Scene 1

(The stage is dark. The play opens with a soft piano sonata in background. Lights up. Nervously watering and plucking her plants is **KATHY** *who is barefoot and wearing a small floral print blouse with a round collar and short skirt.*

There is a KNOCK at the door. She ignores the knock. A moment. Another few KNOCKS get louder. **KATHY** *puts down the watering can, takes a deep breath, crosses the stage, and opens the door. The music stops as* **ELIZABETH**, *her older sister in sexy business attire, impatiently rushes in.)*

ELIZABETH. Hi. What's with you? I was banging out there – couldn't you hear me?

KATHY. No.

> (**KATHY** *peeks outside, and then closes the door as* **ELIZABETH** *brushes by her. She turns.)*

ELIZABETH. Then you must be getting deaf.

KATHY. I still have perfect pitch. I was tested professionally the other day.

ELIZABETH. *(sarcastically)* Thank you.

(taking her coat off)

For that valuable information.

(She tosses her coat on the chair, puts her purse down and runs her hands through her hair. **KATHY** *goes back to her plants.)*

ELIZABETH. *(turns, questioningly)* And what's that funky smell?

KATHY. I think someone egged my car.

ELIZABETH. Yeah, that's it. It reminds me of the time we left eggs boiling and went to a movie. Remember that?

KATHY. Of course I do. Mom got so mad at me.

ELIZABETH. I don't remember that, but we better clean up your car before the mess dries.

KATHY. I don't want to.

ELIZABETH. We have to. That stuff can take the paint off.

KATHY. It's not gonna dry so fast. It's pretty damp tonight.

ELIZABETH. *(goes to the mirror)* Yeah, it sure is. Damn fog – look at my hair. So...

(fixing her hair)

here I am, what's going on.

(turns and looks at her)

You made it sound so serious.

KATHY. It is.

ELIZABETH. And why'd you hang up on me?

*(**KATHY**, turns away from her and picks up her watering can.)*

KATHY. Because you weren't paying attention. You were shuffling papers and talking to other people.

ELIZABETH. I heard everything you said. You left your job and need some legal advice. And then you hung up.

(**KATHY** *walks around watering the plants.* **ELIZABETH** *starts to follow her.*)

ELIZABETH. Which you've never done to me before.

KATHY. You do it and it seems effective.

ELIZABETH. *(laughs)* Not a good idea to copy everything I do, little sister. Were you really fired?

KATHY. Technically I resigned. But they suggested I do so for my own sake.

ELIZABETH. What happened?

KATHY. Wait a sec. Let me finish this.

(She picks up her little rake and loosens the soil of one of her plants thoughtfully.)

ELIZABETH. *(impatiently)* Kathy, come on. I need to lock up one of the studios tonight.

KATHY. Alright.

(still digging)

It all started at the beginning of the year when –

(Elizabeth's cell phone RINGS and she puts her hand up authoritatively, as in "stop.")

ELIZABETH. *(interrupting)* Let me just see who this is. I'm short two people.

(**KATHY** *turns away and heads to another plant.* **ELIZABETH** *rushes to her purse, takes out her cell phone and looks at it...*)

ELIZABETH. *(thinks)* Not important.

(puts it down)

Now, you were saying...

KATHY. You're always in a hurry.

(She slowly waters a plant in silence.)

ELIZABETH. *(rolls her eyes)* You know, most plants die of over watering. Root rot.

KATHY. Don't lecture me about flora. Remember, I'm the one who won the botany award.

(**ELIZABETH** *grabs a chair and sits down. She tries/pretends to relax.*)

ELIZABETH. You certainly did. In the 6th grade.

KATHY. That's right. It was the year you won the dance contest. And the math ribbon.

ELIZABETH. I can't believe you remember that stuff.

(**KATHY** *puts the watering can down on the table.* **ELIZABETH** *casually looks around and stares at the stack of magazines on the chair. She jumps up, picks up some magazines and reads the covers angrily.*)

ELIZABETH. I see Mom's been over lately.

(*tosses down some magazines*)

Field and Stream? Bon Appetite?

(*She rifles through more. And holds one up.*)

ELIZABETH. Ebony?

(**ELIZABETH** *angrily flings it down.*)

ELIZABETH. Why didn't you tell me she's going for that scam again.

KATHY. She hasn't been buying that many.

ELIZABETH. Don't you understand? She's going through all her money on these contests.

KATHY. She said she subscribed to some of them for me.

ELIZABETH. And you believe that?

(**ELIZABETH** *goes back to the pile and looks at one.*)

ELIZABETH. Any good articles this month in "Bowhunting Magazine"?

(**KATHY** *looks down and doesn't answer.*)

ELIZABETH. (*frustrated*) Damn. Now I've gotta handle her craziness again. Like I don't have enough to do.

(*sits down in a heap*)

Listen. I have a business to run and you better start telling me what your problem is so I can fix it.

KATHY. I don't think you can. I might need an attorney.

ELIZABETH. You said that earlier. Done. Lucky for you I have a lawyer friend handy. He'll nip this thing in the bud. But what could you be getting sued for?

KATHY. I didn't say I was getting sued.

(**KATHY** *wanders and straightens up the magazines, placing them carefully on the table.*)

ELIZABETH. Well, that's what I told him anyway. And he agreed to stop by.

KATHY. Now?

ELIZABETH. Yes, now. I was giving him a dance lesson when you called. He's coming over after he drops his daughter off.

KATHY. *(angry)* I need to talk to you first. Not a stranger. This is very personal.

ELIZABETH. You shouldn't be uncomfortable, he's helped me before.

KATHY. *(still upset)* I wish you would have asked me first.

ELIZABETH. *(patiently)* I'm sorry. The timing was too perfect, we were supposed to have dinner tonight.

(**KATHY** *sits down at the table surprised.*)

KATHY. Is he your boyfriend?

ELIZABETH. No, he's just a friend. You know I don't do the boyfriend thing.

KATHY. What's he like?

ELIZABETH. *(sharply)* He'll help us – that's what he's like.

KATHY. *(softly)* I want to know what he's like.

(*Visibly aggravated,* **ELIZABETH** *slowly takes a deep breath.*)

ELIZABETH. Fine. Edward's a nice man, a little boring, but very smart. Divorced. His daughter's been taking modern jazz for a long time and recently he started taking some dance lessons, privately, from me.

KATHY. What kind of dance lessons?

(**ELIZABETH** *looks at her with disbelief.* **KATHY** *looks back* *at her, waiting.* **ELIZABETH** *tries to keep composed.*)

ELIZABETH. Ballroom, alright? We were doing the box step when you called.

(*she leans forward*)

And whatever you did, Edward could write a very intimidating letter on his stationery and get you your job back. So what's the big problem?

KATHY. The term is inappropriate behavior.

ELIZABETH. (*smiles*) You finally told off that pompous principal?

KATHY. (*taken aback*) No. Nothing like that.

(**KATHY** *thinks and doesn't answer for a moment.* **ELIZABETH** *is waiting.*)

KATHY. My throat is dry. Do ya want something to drink?

ELIZABETH. What do you have?

(**KATHY** *gets up and heads to the refrigerator.*)

KATHY. I just bought some orange soda. I have milk, or lots of beer.

ELIZABETH. (*wincing*) Actually, I'm fine. Have you told Mom any of this yet?

(**KATHY** *ignores her and brings out a large bottle of orange soda and pours a glass. She sits back down.*)

ELIZABETH. Well? What was the big "inappropriate" behavior?

KATHY. I hope you understand. And I think you will. You see, over this past year, I've been fortunate to have met...

(*There is a loud KNOCK at the door and they both turn.* **ELIZABETH** *pops up.*)

ELIZABETH. Hold that thought – must be Edward. He sure made it here quickly. I'll let him in.

(*turns and faces* **KATHY**)

And now you can tell both of us what happened at the

same time.

(**KATHY** *grabs the watering can and gets up.* **ELIZABETH** *glides to the door and opens it. To her surprise, it is* **TONY**, *the hip art teacher who works with Kathy. Tony is wearing khaki pants, a long sleeve button down shirt with rolled up sleeves, vest and sneakers. He comes in sheepishly carrying a cardboard box.*)

TONY. Hey. Is Kathy here?

ELIZABETH. And you are...?

(**KATHY** *turns around and sees him.*)

KATHY. Tony?

TONY. Whoa Kathy! I felt so badly when I heard what happened. Are you okay?

KATHY. Not really.

(**KATHY** *sits back down.* **ELIZABETH** *looks at the box...*)

ELIZABETH. Can I help you with something?

TONY. Kathy left so quickly she didn't take all of her things. I boxed them up before people started going through them.

(**KATHY** *looks at him and sips her orange soda.*)

KATHY. Thank you.

TONY. No problemo. And I have your jacket in the car. So... Where should I put this?

(**KATHY** *doesn't respond and stares into space.* **TONY** *still stands there with the box.*)

ELIZABETH. *(loudly)* Kathy? Where do you want the box?

KATHY. *(points)* My bedroom. Over there.

(**TONY** *nods and exits.* **ELIZABETH** *turns to* **KATHY** *and whispers.*)

ELIZABETH. Who's this guy?

KATHY. The art teacher. He's my best friend.

ELIZABETH. *(with a wink)* Is he your "inappropriate behavior?"

KATHY. No.

(TONY walks back into the room. Now ELIZABETH smiles at him.)

TONY. I put the box on your bed, if that's okay. Nice place.

KATHY. Thanks, Tony.

ELIZABETH. *(charmingly)* Yes, Tony. Thank you for being so kind. I'm Kathy's older sister, Elizabeth. She tells me you work at the school, too.

TONY. Yep.

(He goes to shake her hand.)

TONY. Tony Knight.

(They shake)

I teach art. But my first love is making music. Kathy and I jam together sometimes. She's really good on those keys.

ELIZABETH. And you play...?

TONY. Guitar and banjo.

ELIZABETH. Nice to meet you. Any friend of my sister's, is a friend of mine.

(He awkwardly smiles.)

TONY. *(to **KATHY**)* The police came.

*(**KATHY** doesn't respond.)*

ELIZABETH. *(surprised)* The police?

TONY. *(motioning towards **ELIZABETH**)* You haven't told her yet?

KATHY. She just got here. Did you see Sal?

TONY. He wasn't around.

KATHY. I can't reach him. I hope he's okay.

ELIZABETH. Sal?

KATHY. *(quite matter of fact)* Salvatore.

*(There is a KNOCK at the door. **KATHY** grabs the water can and gets up nervously to tend to her plants again. **ELIZABETH** lets loose and yells...)*

ELIZABETH. It's open!

EDWARD. (OS) Elizabeth?

ELIZABETH. *(shouting)* Yes. Just come in!

(**EDWARD** *enters wearing a conservative suit.* **ELIZABETH** *looks at him and he smiles. He obviously likes her.*)

EDWARD. Good. I wasn't sure this was the apartment. It's so foggy I couldn't see the address on the curb.

(*She walks over to him, gives him a formal, but friendly hug, and shows him in.*)

ELIZABETH. Hope my directions were clear.

EDWARD. Yes, quite easy for me to follow. I guess I'm a better driver than dancer.

ELIZABETH. *(smiles)* You're doing fine.

(**ELIZABETH** *turns to everyone.*)

ELIZABETH. This is my friend, Edward. He's an attorney – he's here to help us, Kathy. And...

(*points to* **TONY**)

That's Tony, Kathy's friend who just dropped by.

TONY. *(to* **EDWARD***)* Hey. *(gets up)* Kathy, I'll go get the rest of your stuff from my car.

(**TONY** *exits.*)

ELIZABETH. Kathy, come sit down.

(*She pats the sofa.* **KATHY** *sits where she's told.*)

ELIZABETH. Ed, Can I get you something to drink? *(thinking)* Oh, or maybe...

EDWARD. *(sits)* No thanks, I'm good. *(smiles)* I have a full schedule lately, but I would always make time to help your family.

(**ELIZABETH** *sits next to* **KATHY** *who is awkwardly in between* **ELIZABETH** *and* **EDWARD**.)

ELIZABETH. Thanks, Ed. Kathy and I appreciate you coming. We realize you're a very busy man.

(**KATHY** *doesn't respond.* **ELIZABETH** *nudges her.*)

EDWARD. *(to Kathy)* Elizabeth has done a lot for Bunny over these past years. So, just fill me in.

ELIZABETH. Alright. Kathy will just...fill you in.

(*There is a silence.* **EDWARD** *starts to look at* **ELIZABETH** *and* **KATHY** *questioningly.*)

ELIZABETH. *(sternly)* We're here to help you, Kathy, and Edward is a busy man. So please tell us why we're here.

(**KATHY** *looks at them. The front door opens as* **TONY** *reenters with a jacket.*)

TONY. Do you want this in the bedroom, too?

KATHY. *(popping up)* I'll show you where to put it.

(**KATHY** *grabs the cell phone off the table and leads* **TONY** *off-stage to the bedroom.*)

ELIZABETH. *(whispering)* My sister has always been a bit socially awkward.

EDWARD. *(thinking of something nice to say)* She has a cute apartment.

ELIZABETH. It works for her. My mother lives around here, too.

EDWARD. Is that a good or a bad thing?

ELIZABETH. *(rises)* It would drive me crazy, but Kathy seems to like it.

(**EDWARD** *nods.* **KATHY** *and* **TONY** *come back in and sit on the sofa.*)

ELIZABETH. Now let's see. Kitty, I mean Kathy, teaches, or taught... music at the middle school a few blocks away.

(*No response as everybody looks at* **ELIZABETH**.)

ELIZABETH. And...it was very nice of Tony to get your things. He teaches art there. Thank you, Tony.

TONY. You're welcome.

(**TONY** *gets up to leave.*)

KATHY. Don't go, Tony. Please stay. Can you?

TONY. *(shrugging)* I guess.

(**KATHY** *smiles and relaxes a little.* **TONY** *sits back down.* **ELIZABETH** *is frustrated.*)

ELIZABETH. Alright. You said you have some beer in the fridge. Anybody want one?

TONY. I'll take one, thanks.

(*No one else responds,* **ELIZABETH** *gets two beers, and hands one to* **TONY**. *She sits, opens hers, and takes a gulp.* **EDWARD** *is eagerly awaiting the problem and leans forward. Silence.*)

EDWARD. *(trying)* So, Kathy, you teach music?

ELIZABETH. Yes. Kathy's a music teacher, and Tony's an art teacher.

(**TONY** *loudly POPS open his beer. Starts drumming the table.*)

TONY. *(playfully, to* **KATHY**) And Elizabeth is a dance teacher, and Edward teaches us… the law.

(**KATHY** *giggles.* **ELIZABETH** *gives them a dirty look.*)

KATHY. *(quietly)* Did anybody hear me mention Sal?

ELIZABETH. *(impatient)* Yes. And you mentioned Sal or Salvatore. Is he a teacher, too?

KATHY. No. He doesn't teach.

ELIZABETH. Alright, now we know that there is a Sal. But he doesn't teach.

KATHY. Actually Sal doesn't have a job. He's a student.

(*She stops abruptly, and she exchanges glances with* **TONY**. *A moment.*)

KATHY. *(matter-of-fact)* And the administration is upset about my relationship with him.

ELIZABETH. With who, Sal? The student?

KATHY. Yes.

EDWARD. *(calmly)* And how would you describe this relationship?

KATHY. *(thinking)* Close. We are very close.

ELIZABETH. Were you giving him preferential treatment?

KATHY. I don't think so.

EDWARD. *(knowingly)* Kathy, how old is Sal?

KATHY. 13.

EDWARD. And you're fond of this boy?

(**KATHY** *never makes eye contact with* **EDWARD**.)

KATHY. Very much so. We have a special relationship.

EDWARD. And who knew about this relationship?

ELIZABETH. *(scoffing)* Relationship?

KATHY. Nobody. We weren't ready to tell anyone. Sal's mother somehow found out and called the principal. I don't know who told her.

TONY. *(quickly)* Kathy, I heard that one of Sal's friends told his parents. That's how it got out.

KATHY. *(belligerent)* I don't believe that. Sal wouldn't tell anybody.

ELIZABETH. Wouldn't tell anybody what?

KATHY. That we're in a relationship. A committed one.

(**EDWARD** *looks away and* **ELIZABETH** *is stunned as it takes a moment to register.*)

ELIZABETH. *(incredulous)* What? Jesus, Kathy – you must be kidding!

KATHY. I'm not kidding.

ELIZABETH. He's 13! And one of your students!

(**ELIZABETH** *looks at* **KATHY** *in horror.* **KATHY** *glares back at her.*)

KATHY. Sal's a great human being and incredibly mature for his age.

(**ELIZABETH** *can't contain herself and jumps up.*)

ELIZABETH. You've gone nuts!

KATHY. You don't know him. Tony, tell them about Sal. Please?

(She looks pleadingly at **TONY**. *He is uncomfortable.)*

TONY. Me?

*(***KATHY*** continues to look at him.)*

TONY. Okay. Well...

(drinks his beer)

Sal is a really good kid. Nice boy. And quite talented musically.

KATHY. He's brilliant.

ELIZABETH. Tony, do you approve of this?

*(***TONY*** looks at* **KATHY** *and then looks down.)*

TONY. *(looks down)* Kathy's been a good friend to me these past years.

ELIZABETH. *(turns to* **KATHY***)* Does Mom know about this?

*(***KATHY*** fidgets in her chair.)*

ELIZABETH. You better call her right now and tell her everything. If she hears about this through the grapevine she'll have a heart attack.

KATHY. *(defensively)* I told her a few months ago that I finally found somebody special. And I told her last week who he was but she didn't say anything.

ELIZABETH. Then she probably wasn't listening.

*(***ELIZABETH*** sits down. Covers her face with her hands.* **EDWARD** *becomes professional.)*

EDWARD. Tell me, Kathy. How do you think this affair became public?

KATHY. I don't know.

ELIZABETH. *(in disbelief)* The affair? Let's not make this worse than it is!

KATHY. Elizabeth, please at least try to understand my feelings.

*(***EDWARD*** looks at* **ELIZABETH**. **ELIZABETH** *gets up and walks away.)*

TONY. I have some info, Kathy. Wanna hear?

(**KATHY** *nods, yes.* **EDWARD** *listens.* **TONY** *finishes his beer.*)

TONY. I heard that Sal's mother found out and when Sal was questioned by her he admitted everything. She called the principal.

(*A moment of silence.* **KATHY** *is confused.*)

EDWARD. Thank you, Tony.

TONY. (*turns to* **EDWARD**) I want to help. Kathy's always been on my side when I've had brushes with the faculty.

(**ELIZABETH** *comes back to the table. No one speaks.*)

TONY. (*babbling*) Just last week Kathy was the only member of the staff who supported me when I wanted to bring a local art exhibit to the school. Because it was different, the administration was against it. And with Kathy's help we set up the...

(**ELIZABETH** *waves him off.*)

ELIZABETH. (*interrupting*) Kathy? You haven't done anything weird with this kid, have you?

KATHY. I wouldn't do anything weird.

EDWARD. Weird is not the right word. Kathy, I need to ask you something. I know it's none of our business, but this will come up. Were you physically close with Sal?

KATHY. Yes.

ELIZABETH. (*plugging her ears*) This is too crazy for me.

KATHY. (*angry*) Biz, don't be like that. You can't control who you fall in love with.

(**ELIZABETH** *winces again and tries to gain her composure. She starts pacing.*)

ELIZABETH. You're in big trouble.

(*Edward's cell phone vibrates and he pulls it out and looks at it.* **TONY** *gets up. There is a moment.*)

TONY. I think I better say goodbye.

ELIZABETH. Goodbye Tony. Thanks again for coming.

KATHY. (*rising*) Tony, please don't go. It's easier with you here.

(TONY sits back down, KATHY sits next to him. EDWARD puts his cell phone away.)

ELIZABETH. I don't know what we're gonna do.

KATHY. Biz, you're only looking at the superficial fact that he's 13 and I'm older.

EDWARD. Yes, but that superficial fact is a felony. I assume the police have been contacted?

TONY. Yes. And the principal told Kathy to go home and stay there.

EDWARD. Kathy, don't misunderstand our questions, we need all the facts so we can help you.

ELIZABETH. *(sighing)* Oh God, I need to think.

(rubbing her temples)

Kathy, why don't you go to your room and call Mom before she hears anything. I mean it, call her right now and explain, or there will be fireworks later. And go change…Clean yourself up a little.

(KATHY gives her a look, gets up and storms off towards the bedroom. TONY gets up.)

EDWARD. Tony, if you don't mind, could you please stay for another minute. I want to ask you a few things. I'm a little in the dark about all this.

TONY. I can stay if you want me to.

ELIZABETH. Apparently Edward does, Tony. So… another beer perhaps?

TONY. Sure.

(TONY sits back down. ELIZABETH, disgustedly, gets him another beer. She sits down and listens.)

EDWARD. Is this the first time your school has had this problem?

TONY. I think so. Or no one's been caught recently.

EDWARD. You think this goes on?

ELIZABETH. I've never heard about a female teacher falling for a young student except on the news.

TONY. It is more common for male teachers to have their eye on some of the senior girls. One of my frat brothers who coached high school was caught with his track star.

EDWARD. A female?

TONY. Yes.

EDWARD. How old was she?

TONY. He was 24 and she was 16 at the time. It went to trial.

EDWARD. *(curious)* How did the court rule?

TONY. He had to do jail time and register as a sex offender. It ruined his life.

ELIZABETH. Edward, this conversation is a waste of time.

TONY. *(a bit belligerent)* The female student testified that it was consensual. But it was still considered rape and child molestation.

ELIZABETH. *(disgusted)* This isn't similar at all. Kathy's not some sexual predator, she's in love.

TONY. The girl told the court she loved him and wanted to get married.

(**ELIZABETH** *shakes her head in disgust.*)

EDWARD. Elizabeth, the cases are comparable. Your sister is going to face some very serious charges.

ELIZABETH. Come on, this is completely different from that sort of thing. How could a young girl refuse a big intimidating jock... in a power position.

(stands up)

My sister is just a sensitive girl. I bet Sal took advantage of HER to brag to his friends.

EDWARD. I'm afraid due to Sal's age, whatever the relationship, it is still child abuse according to the law.

(**EDWARD** *stands up and pulls out his cell phone again. He sees who's calling him and puts it back in his pocket while* **TONY** *speaks...*)

TONY. But there are double standards.

ELIZABETH. These aren't double standards. My sister didn't sexually assault anyone. Women can't rape men.

TONY. I bet if Kathy was a guy, she'd be tarred and feathered even before the trial.

ELIZABETH. *(dismissive)* Is that what you want for Kathy, Tony?

TONY. No, of course not.

ELIZABETH. Tony, I think Edward and I can take it from here.

TONY. I'm sorry. Of course I don't want Kathy to get hurt.

EDWARD. *(firmly)* Elizabeth, please let me finish. I want Tony's perspective of Kathy.

(**ELIZABETH** *sits back down, annoyed.*)

TONY. You mean what's she like?

EDWARD. Yes. Your impressions.

TONY. Okay. *(thinking)* She's really smart, and very sweet. She's a good musician, a good teacher. She relates well to the kids, *(pause)* better than to adults, actually. She always gets stressed at open house having to deal with the parents.

(further ruminating)

Our bond is that I'm a bit of an outsider, myself, most people don't understand that my art forms express...

ELIZABETH. *(interrupting)* So what's that little Don Juan like? Does he try to seduce all the female teachers?

TONY. No, I don't think it's like that at all. Sally, Sal – is a very serious boy. Kathy recognized his talent and started spending extra time with him, working on music. They composed together.

ELIZABETH. *(emotionally)* They certainly did. And it obviously got out of hand. Kitty was sure manipulated, or she's gone insane.

EDWARD. *(uncomfortable)* Alright, thank you, Tony. You've been very helpful.

(**TONY** *starts to get up.*)

TONY. I'm sorry all this had to happen. If there's anything more I can do just let me know.

ELIZABETH. *(fake smile)* Thank you, we will.

EDWARD. There is something you can help us with. If you find out any more information or hear anything important, please let us know so we can be prepared.

*(**EDWARD** stands, reaches into his briefcase and hands him a business card. **TONY** looks at it and nods his head. **ELIZABETH** heads to the door and opens it.)*

TONY. I promise. And say goodbye to Kathy for me.

*(**TONY** turns to leave.)*

EDWARD. Again, thank you for your thoughts and patience. You realize that this is a very difficult time.

*(**TONY** waves and exits. **ELIZABETH** returns to her chair.)*

ELIZABETH. Kathy is the victim here. That little Romeo is now probably the most popular guy at school.

EDWARD. Elizabeth, you need to face the facts, your sister may have committed a crime.

ELIZABETH. *(rises and paces)* Damn, Edward. Is it a crime to be an immature, hopeless romantic? Who happens to have gone a little nuts?

EDWARD. No. But statutory rape and sexual battery by an authority figure is. This is not my specialty. Truthfully, if this goes to trial I may have to refer you to another attorney.

ELIZABETH. I hope that doesn't happen.

*(There is a silence and **ELIZABETH**, upset, sits back down. **EDWARD** sits next to her.)*

EDWARD. Has Kathy always had a self-esteem problem?

ELIZABETH. *(sharply)* She's shy. I don't know about her self-esteem.

EDWARD. I'm asking these questions for a reason – I'm trying to get to know her. She never once looked me in the eye.

ELIZABETH. *(apologetically)* I know, I know. I guess she's insecure. What else?

EDWARD. When you were growing up. Did she have friends? Was she happy?

ELIZABETH. *(thinking)* I don't know. She was always pretty immature. Didn't have many friends, I guess.

EDWARD. Boyfriends?

ELIZABETH. Not that I remember, really.

EDWARD. I haven't heard much about your father.

ELIZABETH. There isn't much to tell. He died awhile ago.

EDWARD. Did Kathy have a good relationship with him?

ELIZABETH. My parents divorced when I was young and he moved away. Why do you ask?

EDWARD. I'm just trying to figure all this out. We might have to build a case.

ELIZABETH. You're going down the wrong path, there. No sex abuse. My mom raised us most of our lives.

EDWARD. I see. Your mother had it pretty rough, then.

*(**ELIZABETH** gets up and crosses to the mirror. Fixes her hair.)*

ELIZABETH. Yes. She had to work full time and take care of us. I guess she did her best. *(a moment)* And when she wasn't working, cooking or cleaning, she was busy praying.

*(Edward's cell phone vibrates, he pulls it out of his pocket and checks who's calling him. He decides to answer and holds a finger up to **ELIZABETH** indicating "excuse me." He then stands and walks downstage.)*

EDWARD. *(into phone)* Yes Patty, what is it? *(listens intently)* Sure, go. I'll take them to dinner Monday night. *(nodding)* No problem, I'd love to. I'll be there by 6. *(earnestly)* I said by 6, nothing will come up. *(getting angry)* Patty, I said I'll be there at 6. Can't you let go of that already? *(quietly)* Now I'm in a meeting, goodbye.

(He hangs up, shoves the phone back in his pocket, and

collects himself.)

EDWARD. *(deep breath)* Alright, so, ah... yes, your Mother worked and prayed. *(focussing)* It's a wonder you both were able to go to college.

(He approaches her.)

ELIZABETH. We had to work the whole time. I had wanted to be a dancer but I couldn't afford to dream so I took business classes along with theatre arts. Kitty continued her music but went into education.

EDWARD. Seems like you did okay for yourself.

ELIZABETH. I worked my ass off.

*(**ELIZABETH** crosses to the sofa.)*

EDWARD. Yes, and it's very admirable.

(She turns and looks at him.)

EDWARD. *(clumsily)* Your success. Four prosperous dance and exercise studios. *(tentatively)* I guess you never had time to get married.

ELIZABETH. Marriage is a crap shoot – and I'm not a gambler.

(sitting down)

So, you wanted to know about Kathy – I think we're getting off the subject. *(business-like)* Is there anything else you need to know?

*(It is obvious that **ELIZABETH** wants this conversation to be over.)*

EDWARD. Not really. And, I'm sorry – didn't mean to pry. I was just trying to get the whole picture.

ELIZABETH. One thing you should know. Kathy's always had a vivid imagination. Maybe she didn't really do anything with that boy.

EDWARD. Could be.

ELIZABETH. But whatever happened, it had to be consensual.

EDWARD. *(sighs)* It's never considered consensual when one party is much older and the other party is a minor. Tony was right, let's be glad she's not a male.

ELIZABETH. Do you think there's a double standard?

EDWARD. Yes, but for once it works in your favor. And we need to be practical and take advantage of everything.

(There is a moment. **KATHY** *comes into the kitchen wearing black pants, pink shirt, pumps, and long chunky necklaces.* **EDWARD** *glances at her.)*

EDWARD. And now, I think I'm ready for that beer, thank you.

*(***ELIZABETH** *gets up, goes to the fridge, and hands* **EDWARD** *a beer.)*

KATHY. Did Tony leave?

ELIZABETH. Yes. He had to get home. Nice guy. And he said to tell you goodbye.

KATHY. I wish he hadn't left.

ELIZABETH. Did you call Mom?

KATHY. Yes, so I changed. She's on her way over. She didn't say much.

ELIZABETH. Oh, she'll respond all right, she probably wasn't really listening for a change. Give her time to process the information.

(Agitated, **KATHY** *sits down. She pulls her cell phone out of her pocket and looks at it.)*

ELIZABETH. Give me that phone. We don't want to talk to anybody.

*(***ELIZABETH** *grabs Kathy's cell phone, turns it off and puts it down.)*

EDWARD. Kathy, there are still a few facts we need to know before we plan some type of strategy.

KATHY. I thought Tony told you everything.

ELIZABETH. Not exactly. There are certain activities I, we, want to hear about directly from you.

KATHY. Okay.

(ELIZABETH *looks at* EDWARD. EDWARD *takes out a notebook and pen from his briefcase.*)

EDWARD. Kathy, have you had sex with Sal?

KATHY. *(matter-of-fact)* Yes.

ELIZABETH. Sex? Real sex?

KATHY. Yes, Biz, real sex. It's time you get it. We're a couple, we're in love.

EDWARD. More than once?

KATHY. Yes.

(EDWARD *jots down notes.*)

ELIZABETH. Where the hell did you do it? In the classroom?

KATHY. No. Never at school. A few times here. Mostly in my car. The backseat.

ELIZABETH. Your little Mustang?

KATHY. There's plenty of room if you push the seats completely forward. He's not that tall...yet.

(A silence.)

ELIZABETH. *(shaking her head)* Weren't you afraid of being spotted?

KATHY. No. When we worked on the music arrangements for the assemblies, I would drive him home. There's a real secluded area on the way.

EDWARD. Alright, we needed to know that. Thank you for your honesty.

(There is a loud, authoritative BANG BANG at the door. EDWARD *looks at* ELIZABETH, *concerned.* ELIZABETH *jumps up.)*

ELIZABETH. I'll get it.

(KATHY *scurries offstage to her bedroom.* ELIZABETH *opens the door and their mother,* MARILYN *enters wearing boots, spandex leggings, a colorful blouse, wide belt, muffler, and too many necklaces.)*

MARILYN. Elizabeth? What are you doing here?

ELIZABETH. I came to help Kathy.

MARILYN. *(calmly)* You didn't have to. I can take care of this foolishness.

ELIZABETH. Did Kathy explain everything to you?

MARILYN. I heard enough. And it sounds like one big misunderstanding.

(shakes head in denial)

But it certainly is nice to see you, honey. It's been a couple of weeks.

(She tries to give **ELIZABETH** *a kiss as* **ELIZABETH** *backs off, she then notices* **EDWARD**.*)*

*(***EDWARD** *puts his notebook away.)*

MARILYN. Oh...we have company?

ELIZABETH. Mom, this is Edward. He's a friend of mine who happens to be an attorney. I took the liberty of asking him to come over to help us out.

MARILYN. *(flirtatiously)* Is he your boyfriend?

ELIZABETH. *(sharply)* He's a friend, and that's all you need to know.

MARILYN. My goodness – don't get so touchy. Would having a boyfriend be such a crime? Where is she? *(loudly calling)* Kitty?

*(***ELIZABETH** *turns around and realizes that* **KATHY** *has left the room.)*

ELIZABETH. She's changing, I guess. I'll go get her.

*(***ELIZABETH** *exits,* **MARILYN** *looks around, eyes* **EDWARD**, *and takes a seat too close to him.)*

MARILYN. So very glad to meet you, but I don't think we'll be needing a lawyer. I'm sure this is a terrible mistake. Kitty has always had an active imagination.

(She looks **EDWARD** *over.)*

MARILYN. *(smiling)* Now isn't that a nice tie.

(She touches it gently and he tries to back away.)

EDWARD. Thank you. It's Italian. My kids gave it to me for Father's Day.

MARILYN. *(disappointed)* Oh. How nice that you have children.

(She gets up and goes over to the mirror adjusting her hair.)

EDWARD. *(proudly)* Yes, twins. A boy and a girl.

MARILYN. Twins. That must be a lot of work for your wife.

EDWARD. I've been divorced five years.

(She turns around and comes back to the sofa.)

MARILYN. *(happier)* Divorced? I'm so sorry to hear that.

(sits again)

And how do you know Elizabeth?

EDWARD. My daughter, Bunny, goes to her dance studio. She's been taking lessons there for quite some time.

(ELIZABETH *comes back into the room. She looks at* **EDWARD** *and rolls her eyes.)*

ELIZABETH. Mom, Kathy's straightening up. She'll be out in a minute.

MARILYN. That's fine. I'm enjoying getting to know your… "friend."

(ELIZABETH *turns around and mouths "I'm sorry" to* **EDWARD**. *He tries to pick up a magazine,* **MARILYN** *touches his jacket.)*

MARILYN. That's a pretty sharp suit you have on. Italian, also?

EDWARD. I believe it is. You have quite a good eye.

MARILYN. I used to work in the fashion industry.

ELIZABETH. Mom was employed at J. C. Penney's for many years.

MARILYN. *(defensively)* I was the manager of women's wear.

EDWARD. It must have been very difficult working full time and raising the girls.

MARILYN. It wasn't easy, but I got through it, with our Lord's help.

(Not wanting to be in this conversation, ELIZABETH heads to the bedroom.)

ELIZABETH. *(shaking her head)* I'll go check on Kathy.

(She exits.)

MARILYN. I retired several years ago.

EDWARD. Good for you. I hope you're enjoying yourself.

MARILYN. I will soon. I plan on doing some traveling which is something I haven't been able to do. I'm coming into quite a bit of money soon.

EDWARD. Oh really? How nice for you.

(She turns to make sure ELIZABETH can't hear.)

MARILYN. *(quietly)* Yes, it's very exciting. I've entered this new contest and I've been assured I'm a winner. Don't tell Elizabeth, she doesn't approve of anything I do to try to get ahead.

EDWARD. How did you find this contest?

MARILYN. It was on the internet. Kathy gave me her old computer and I finally found it to be good for something.

EDWARD. *(holding up a magazine)* Does it have anything to do with magazines?

MARILYN. A little bit.

EDWARD. Good luck.

MARILYN. Thank you. You can pray for me if you're so inclined.

*(**EDWARD** doesn't answer but respectfully smiles. A pause. **MARILYN** looks at him carefully...)*

MARILYN. What did you say your name was?

EDWARD. Edward.

MARILYN. Yes. Edward...?

(Nodding that she wants more.)

EDWARD. Green. Ed Green.

MARILYN. *(thinking)* Green. That's a nice name. That's it? Anything on the end of it?

EDWARD. What do you mean, like an "e"?

MARILYN. Yes, or…

EDWARD. No. It's just Green. Like the color.

MARILYN. I see. Like the color. *(pause)* I was just wondering if it was always that plain, or maybe it was shortened. You know, for…… simplicity.

EDWARD. Shortened? You mean something like Green – berg, perhaps?

(**MARILYN** *just looks at him, waiting for an answer.*)

EDWARD. Nope. It was always Green. Just plain green.

MARILYN. *(smiling)* I love the color green.

(*An awkward moment.* **EDWARD** *spots an insect moving on Marilyn's chair.*)

EDWARD. Hope you're not afraid of spiders. There's quite a big one on your chair.

MARILYN. Oh my, I am!

(**MARILYN** *jumps up.*)

MARILYN. *(shaking)* Eeey! I hate spiders.

(**EDWARD** *gets up, grabbing a magazine.*)

EDWARD. I'll get it. *(to himself)* These magazines are coming in handy.

MARILYN. No! I can't abide harming any of God's creatures. Please try to capture it and put it outside – where it belongs.

(**EDWARD**, *not knowing how, pretends to try to capture it.*)

EDWARD. *(fumbling)* Oh, I'm sorry. It got away. I think it was headed for the door – let me open it real quick.

(*He goes to the front door, opens it, fans the air with the magazine and closes it.*)

MARILYN. Each one of God's creatures is precious.

(**MARILYN** *spots the spider on the floor… coming towards* *her. She lifts her leg and viciously STOMPS on it.*

EDWARD, *startled, turns...)*

MARILYN. *(embarrassed)* But we have dominion over them.

(composing herself)

I think it was a brown recluse spider. They're deadly, you know.

*(***EDWARD** *looks at the floor and back at her. He takes out a tissue from his back pocket.)*

EDWARD. *(awkwardly)* I'll clean it up.

(He reaches down and wipes up the spider, looks around and finds a trash can.)

MARILYN. *(sweetly)* Thank you.

(He then nervously sits down again. **MARILYN** *sits down next to him, much too close for comfort. He looks at the bedroom door and stands.)*

EDWARD. I wonder what's taking them so long?

MARILYN. *(loudly)* Kitty? Elizabeth?

*(***ELIZABETH** *enters the room basically pulling* **KATHY** *with her.)*

MARILYN. Here they are. Elizabeth, it was rude to keep your boyfriend waiting.

ELIZABETH. I told you, he's...

(She stops herself, shakes her head, looks at **KATHY** *and prods her.* **KATHY** *steps forward.)*

KATHY. Hi Mom.

(She walks over to **MARILYN** *who smiles and lets* **KATHY** *kiss her.)*

MARILYN. Now what is all this nonsense, Kitty?

(No one speaks. **ELIZABETH** *looks at* **EDWARD** *for help. He looks down.)*

MARILYN. Were you really fired from your job? You've been there eight years, they can't do that to you.

KATHY. Actually I resigned.

ELIZABETH. Kathy was forced to resign. This is a very serious matter which is why Edward is here.

MARILYN. I know, she told me all about it.

ELIZABETH. She did?

KATHY. I didn't do anything terrible, Momma.

(She sits in a chair.)

MARILYN. Of course not. I'm sure it's some sort of misunderstanding.

ELIZABETH. Mother, you're always in denial! Kathy is having an inappropriate relationship. Can't you listen for a change?

MARILYN. I heard every word. She's fallen in love with a wonderful person and he loves her too.

ELIZABETH. And this wonderful person is a student, which happens to be a crime.

KATHY. *(deep breath)* I know it's unusual because of our ages and not great because I'm his teacher and he's my student, but he's brilliant, mature, and we're in love. We're soul mates. God has a plan for all of us, right?

(All is quiet. Marilyn's jaw drops.)

MARILYN. He's your student?

KATHY. Yes.

MARILYN. Katherine? *(gathering herself)* How old is this boy?

KATHY. He's 13, Momma. But he'll be 14 in a few weeks.

*(**MARILYN** gets up and slowly walks over to **KATHY** and sharply SLAPS her across the face. A moment.*

***KATHY** brings her hand up to her face and runs offstage – to her room.*

***ELIZABETH** faces her mother angrily, **EDWARD** looks down embarrassed.)*

ELIZABETH. Jesus, Mom! Just leave!

MARILYN. *(screaming)* And I've told you to watch your language. You're breaking the third commandment!

ELIZABETH. *(screaming back)* Excuse me! How bout... please get your sorry fat ass outa here! Is that better?

(**MARILYN** *stares at her, exhales and takes a seat.*)

ELIZABETH. I'm the one who always has to fix everything. Why do you have my life more difficult!

MARILYN. Lord help us.

ELIZABETH. No, Edward and I are gonna help us. And you're going to go home.

(**MARILYN** *starts to get up, painfully...*)

MARILYN. It's not right. You acting all high and mighty just cause you make good money and have fancy lawyer friends who wear Italian suits and get manicures.

ELIZABETH. I said go...Goodbye!

MARILYN. I'm leaving. But you're breaking the 5th amendment with this attitude.

(**MARILYN** *turns to leave, glances back and stops.*)

MARILYN. And you better apologize real soon or you won't see a dime of that ten million I'll be getting in the next few days.

ELIZABETH. You're not getting any money – it's another scam! You're wasting your savings. How many times do I have to explain that to you. You don't hear what you don't want to hear.

(*As* **MARILYN** *takes a step she buckles over, stumbles, and dramatically grabs her chest.*)

MARILYN. AHHHHH, help...my heart.

(*They turn –* **EDWARD** *approaches, grabs her and helps her to the sofa.*)

ELIZABETH. Shit!

EDWARD. *(panicky)* Are you alright?

(**MARILYN** *doesn't speak but takes some long slow breaths.*)

EDWARD. Liz, Call 9-1-1.

ELIZABETH. No, she's okay. It's not a heart attack.

EDWARD. How do you know? She's having trouble breathing.

(MARILYN flops onto the sofa; ELIZABETH approaches. Edward takes her wrist and checks her pulse.)

ELIZABETH. *(disgustedly)* She'll be okay.

(to MARILYN) Keep your head down, Mom.

(she pushes her head down too roughly)

And breathe slowly.

(turning to EDWARD) Her heart races but it's nerves. She's having a panic attack. It happens all the time.

EDWARD. What can we do for her?

ELIZABETH. She just has to calm down.

(to MARILYN) Mom, did you bring your medication?

MARILYN. Yes. *(taking a breath)* In my purse.

ELIZABETH. Good. I'll get it.

(ELIZABETH gets her mother's purse and rummages through it pulling out a vial. She holds it up.)

ELIZABETH. Is this the one?

MARILYN. Yes. I don't need water.

(She opens the vial.)

ELIZABETH. How many do you need?

(MARILYN holds up one finger. ELIZABETH hands one to her.)

ELIZABETH. Would you like some orange soda? Kathy has some in the house.

(MARILYN swallows a pill, shakes her head "no" and closes her eyes.)

ELIZABETH. Come on. You never know, it might help.

MARILYN. Well, maybe... yes. Orange soda. *(big breath)* Please, sweetheart.

(**ELIZABETH** *grabs a glass, opens the refrigerator and pours her some orange soda.*)

ELIZABETH. Here ya go. Cold, no ice.

MARILYN. *(takes glass)* Thank you. Honey.

EDWARD. Are you sure you wouldn't like to lay down? You might be more comfortable?

MARILYN. No. I'm fine. I'll just rest here for a moment and catch my breath.

(**ELIZABETH** *looks knowingly at* **EDWARD** *and rolls her eyes.*)

ELIZABETH. Of course, Mom. You better stay here and rest. But let's get you into the bedroom.

(**EDWARD** *and* **ELIZABETH** *start to help* **MARILYN** *up... There is a KNOCK at the door. They all turn and put* **MARILYN** *back down.*)

EDWARD. I'll see who it is.

ELIZABETH. Thanks.

(*He walks over, opens it a crack, peeking. Then opens it all the way.*)

EDWARD. Tony?

(**TONY** *rushes in.* **MARILYN** *closes her eyes.*)

TONY. Hi. Excuse me for barging in, but I have some information. Your business card just has your office number, and Kathy isn't answering her phone.

ELIZABETH. I turned it off.

TONY. *(noticing* **MARILYN**) Hey – what happened?

ELIZABETH. Nothing. My mother's having a panic attack – She'll be fine. We were just taking her to the bedroom.

TONY. Okay. Well, I came over cause I just got a phone call from Judith, the drama teacher, and I thought you guys should know... *(whispering)* Unless now's not a good time...

(*He glances at* **MARILYN**.)

ELIZABETH. You can talk. As you can see, she was told what's going on.

EDWARD. Hold your thought Tony, Kathy needs to hear this.

ELIZABETH. I'll tell her to come out and we'll put Mom on her bed. And shut the door.

MARILYN. *(opening one eye)* I'm fine here, I shouldn't be moved.

ELIZABETH. *(firmly)* No, you need it nice and quiet.

(**ELIZABETH** *goes over to the bedroom door.*)

ELIZABETH. Kathy? Will you come out here please? Tony's back and Mom needs to lie down.

(**ELIZABETH** *motions for* **EDWARD** *to bring her mother. He helps her up.*)

ELIZABETH. Kathy?

(There is no answer.)

ELIZABETH. Hold on, Edward.

(**ELIZABETH** *goes offstage to bedroom.* **MARILYN** *tries to shake off* **EDWARD**.)

MARILYN. *(to* **EDWARD**) I'm feeling a little better. I'll be fine right here.

(She sits back down.)

MARILYN. I'll just close my eyes and rest.

(**ELIZABETH** *comes back in.* **MARILYN** *takes some deep breaths.*)

ELIZABETH. Kathy's in the bathroom and can't come out right now. She says she's sick.

(**MARILYN** *closes her eyes.* **EDWARD** *approaches* **ELIZABETH** *and is concerned.*)

EDWARD. Do you think Kathy would hurt herself?

ELIZABETH. Hurt herself?

EDWARD. Yes. There are plenty of sharp objects in the bathroom.

ELIZABETH. Kathy? No. I don't think...

EDWARD. *(interrupting)* Are you sure?

ELIZABETH. *(thinking)* No, I'm not sure about anything anymore.

(**ELIZABETH** and **EDWARD** *rush offstage to the bedroom.* **MARILYN** *opens her eyes and looks at* **TONY**.)

MARILYN. Who are you?

TONY. I teach. At the school with Kathy.

(**MARILYN** *pats the sofa cushion next to her.*)

MARILYN. Tell me, young man. *(pats again)*

(**TONY** *looks at her but doesn't move.*)

MARILYN. Is all this I hear about our Kitty true?

(**TONY** *looks down and doesn't answer.*)

MARILYN. *(more forcefully)* Is there really something going on between my daughter and one of her students?

(**TONY** *still doesn't answer but walks towards the bedroom. Awkward silence.*

ELIZABETH *and* **EDWARD** *come back into the room.*)

TONY. Is she alright?

ELIZABETH. *(to* **TONY***)* Yes. Kathy's out of the bathroom and will join us in a minute.

(**MARILYN** *closes her eyes again.* **ELIZABETH** *can't contain herself.*)

ELIZABETH. Mom, get up. You're going in the bedroom.

(**MARILYN** *opens her eyes.*)

MARILYN. Not necessary. I'm starting to feel better. I'll be leaving in a minute.

ELIZABETH. *(shouts)* Kathy? Hurry up! Tony's waiting.

(**KATHY** *slowly enters.*)

TONY. *(to* **KATHY***)* I've been trying to call you. I promised if I heard something I'd let you guys know.

(*They all look at him.* **MARILYN** *sits up.*)

TONY. Okay. Well, apparently the police were at school for a long time questioning people. And now they're going to be coming here, to your house. Soon... like now.

(*They all look at each other.* **MARILYN** *clutches her hands in prayer.*)

ELIZABETH. Edward, could you please stay a little longer?

(*He looks at her and nods.* **ELIZABETH** *walks over to* **KATHY** *and puts her arm around her.*)

ELIZABETH. I'm so sorry, Kathy. We'll be here and do whatever we can. You know that.

(**KATHY** *walks over to* **TONY.**)

KATHY. Tony? Will you do me a favor? (*softly*) Will you give this message to Sal?

(*She hands him a piece of paper.* **ELIZABETH** *notices and rushes over.*)

ELIZABETH. (*incredulous*) Don't you get it? Are you, crazy? You shouldn't be communicating with him.

EDWARD. Yes, that's not a good idea.

ELIZABETH. Give me that...

(**ELIZABETH** *grabs the note from* **TONY.**)

KATHY. Don't!

ELIZABETH. (*furious*) This has to stop! Now!

KATHY. No!

(**ELIZABETH** *tears up the note.*)

MARILYN. Quiet Kitty! Do what your sister says.

(**KATHY** *runs offstage to her bedroom.*)

TONY. I better leave.

ELIZABETH. Ed? What now?

EDWARD. I don't know.

(**EDWARD** *sits down.*)

EDWARD. Let's all just sit down and try to relax.

ELIZABETH. Isn't there something we can do.

EDWARD. Not at the moment.

ELIZABETH. Then I better call my office and have Karla make up the schedules.

(She goes to her purse and gets out her cell phone.)

MARILYN. *(looking to the sky)* This has to be some kind of mistake.

ELIZABETH. *(viciously)* You told me that God doesn't make mistakes, Mother.

TONY. I think I heard a car door slamming.

MARILYN. *(clutching her chest)* I can do all things through Christ who strengthens me...

(They listen.)

EDWARD. Let's all try to remain calm.

*(**ELIZABETH** just looks at her cell phone. **EDWARD** picks up a ridiculous magazine and thumbs through it. **MARILYN** prays to herself, **TONY** stands awkwardly listening...*

*A KNOCK at the door, everyone freezes. No response. Then several loud KNOCKS. They all look at **ELIZABETH**, who looks at **EDWARD**. He nods. She puts her phone down and doesn't move.)*

ELIZABETH. *(loudly)* Coming!

*(**EDWARD** then rises and turns towards **ELIZABETH**.)*

EDWARD. I will go get the door and you go get Kathy. And try to keep her composed.

*(**EDWARD** turns to approach the door while **ELIZABETH** heads off to the bedroom.)*

MARILYN. *(to **ELIZABETH**)* Honey, I'll go with you.

ELIZABETH. *(threateningly)* No, just sit down! And, you better not say one word...

EDWARD. *(calling)* Be right there.

*(**ELIZABETH** exits to the bedroom. **MARILYN** sits back down. **TONY** hasn't moved. **EDWARD** reaches for the door.)*

TONY. I guess I better leave now.

(**ELIZABETH** *rushes back on-stage.*)

ELIZABETH. Kathy's back in the bathroom. She's throwing up.

(**EDWARD** *steps back, he and* **ELIZABETH** *look at each other.*)

EDWARD. Stay with her. I have to answer the door.

(**EDWARD** *then opens the door part of the way and looks out.*)

EDWARD. So sorry to have kept you waiting.

(*He opens the door the rest of the way and says pleasantly.*)

EDWARD. Hello. Please, come on in.

(*BLACKOUT.*)

END OF ACT 1

ACT 2

Scene 1

(Lights up on Kathy's empty apartment. There is a knock on the door. **KATHY**, *wearing a robe and slippers, appears on stage and approaches the door.)*

KATHY. Who is it?

TONY. (OS) Tony. Can I come in?

KATHY. *(through the closed door)* I'm not supposed to talk to anybody from school.

TONY. (OS) This is different. Dr. Sherman asked me to pick up your music notes for the concert.

*(***KATHY*** swings open the door and they both head to center stage.* **TONY** *has a backpack slung over his shoulder.)*

KATHY. I have rules to follow right now.

TONY. I'm sure, but we need your copy. They don't want to cancel. The kids are ready and the honchos want everything to seem normal.

KATHY. Everything is in a notebook you packed up for me. I'll get it.

*(***KATHY*** makes no attempt to get it.)*

TONY. What happened? Did they take you away?

KATHY. Have you seen Sal?

TONY. *(uncomfortably)* No. And we probably shouldn't be talking about him. *(quietly)* But I did hear that he wouldn't be coming to school for a week or so.

KATHY. Anything else?

TONY. No. Everything is very hush-hush. Hell, I was afraid you'd be in jail.

KATHY. *(getting animated)* I was, and it was pretty scary. I was booked and held most of the night until Elizabeth was able to post bail.

TONY. How much was that?

KATHY. 10 thousand.

TONY. Wow.

KATHY. But she didn't have to pay that. She hired a bail bond company. You pay them a fee, and then they pay the full amount.

TONY. Right. So when's the trial?

KATHY. I don't know. Edward's coming over later to explain.

(**KATHY** *motions for* **TONY** *to sit down.*)

KATHY. I guess you can sit down for a minute.

TONY. Okay. Maybe for a minute.

(*They both sit.*)

KATHY. *(interested)* So who's teaching my class?

TONY. Nobody did today, the kids had a free period. They have a substitute coming tomorrow.

KATHY. Is everybody gossiping?

TONY. No. Like I said, it's not cool to talk about it.

(*They sit for a moment in silence.*)

TONY. I probably should leave.

KATHY. *(slowly gets up)* I'll go get those notes.

(*She exits.* **TONY** *puts his head down until* **KATHY** *reenters. He looks up.*)

TONY. Is there anything you want me to tell the sub tomorrow about the show?

KATHY. No. This is all he or she will need.

(*She hands* **TONY** *the notebook. He puts it in his backpack.*)

KATHY. The students know what to do, just make sure they have plenty of time to warm up.

(A KNOCK is heard at the door.

(She crosses and opens the door. **ELIZABETH** *walks in.)*

KATHY. Hi Biz.

ELIZABETH. Kathy, look at you, you haven't even gotten dressed today. Edward is on his way, why don't you change and brush your hair.

(She notices **TONY** *and is surprised.)*

ELIZABETH. Oh no. This isn't good. At all.

TONY. *(quickly)* I'm just picking up the program for the school concert next week. The principal asked me to stop by and get it.

KATHY. And he just got here.

ELIZABETH. *(relieved)* Alright. I guess that's okay, then.

TONY. And if we didn't have all Kathy's outlines and notations, the Spring show would have to be cancelled.

ELIZABETH. I understand.

(turns to **KATHY***)*

Now go put on some clothes. Go on – I'll see Tony out.

*(***TONY** *gets up.)*

TONY. Good luck, Kathy. Please let me know what's happening.

KATHY. I'll try. But now I have to get dressed... to look good for Edward. Bye.

*(***KATHY** *turns and exits into bedroom.* **TONY** *picks up his backpack and starts to leave.* **ELIZABETH** *waits until* **KATHY** *is gone.)*

ELIZABETH. *(whispering)* Wait, Tony. What have you heard?

TONY. Not much. Just that Sal is very upset and won't be at school for awhile. Students and teachers have been warned that it's not a topic to be discussed.

*(***TONY** *opens the door.)*

TONY. I really want to know what happens to Kathy. Please. And if I can be of any more help, call me.

ELIZABETH. Thank you.

(**TONY** *exits.* **ELIZABETH** *pulls out her cell phone and dials.*)

ELIZABETH. *(into phone)* Hi Dori. I was thinking. How's that piano holding up in Studio B on Genesta? Has it been tuned lately? *(listening)* What time during the day is that room usually available?

(There is a KNOCK. She heads to the door.)

ELIZABETH. *(into phone)* And could you please go to the bank for me? Thanks. Gotta go.

(**ELIZABETH** *hangs up and opens the door.* **MARILYN** *enters with a big shopping bag.*)

ELIZABETH. *(coldly)* We don't need you, Mother. Everything is under control.

MARILYN. Of course. God is in control. Now where is Kitty?

ELIZABETH. Changing her clothes. Edward's coming over.

(**MARILYN** *sits down and sighs. She tries to put the bag out of sight, to hide it.*)

MARILYN. Good. I want to thank him for finding us that nice bail bond company.

ELIZABETH. *(glares at her)* It would have saved me money if we had paid it ourselves.

MARILYN. Honey, ten thousand dollars is a lot of money to write a check for.

ELIZABETH. *(aggravated)* I told you you'd get it back – it's like insurance. If she shows up in court you get the whole amount back. But I had to pay a company to do that and now I'm out a thousand bucks. Which I won't get back.

(**ELIZABETH** *sits, opens her purse and takes out her Blackberry.*)

MARILYN. What makes you think I have that kind of money?

ELIZABETH. I know you do.

MARILYN. How do you know my business?

ELIZABETH. Because when you sold the house, you put 150 grand into your checking account. I know because I told you not to put it there.

MARILYN. That was years ago.

ELIZABETH. Just three. And I know you live mostly on your social security and retirement fund.

(**MARILYN** *walks over to the mirror and fluffs up her hair.*)

MARILYN. Well Miss Fancypants. The way you throw money around I figured a thousand dollars is nothing to you.

ELIZABETH. *(disgusted)* Forget it. I was happy to help Kathy so let's just drop it.

MARILYN. I suppose I would have paid it, if I could have.

ELIZABETH. I said let's drop it!

(**ELIZABETH** *goes back to making notes on her Blackberry.* **MARILYN** *sits.*)

MARILYN. You shouldn't be mad at me.

ELIZABETH. *(shouting)* I'm not mad at you.

MARILYN. Honey, I couldn't pay it if I wanted to. There's hardly any money left in that account.

(**ELIZABETH** *whirls around in shock.*)

ELIZABETH. What?

MARILYN. *(sheepishly)* You heard me.

ELIZABETH. *(incredulous)* I don't believe this. What happened to all of it?

(**MARILYN** *gets up and turns away from her in shame.*)

MARILYN. A real estate venture. I was unlucky.

ELIZABETH. *(stunned)* Unlucky?

MARILYN. Yes, but all that's going to change.

(**ELIZABETH** *walks over to where the shopping bag is and dumps the magazines on the floor.*)

ELIZABETH. *(freaking out)* And these are good investments?

(She then picks up the stack of magazines on the table and slams them down. **MARILYN** *shrinks.* **ELIZABETH** *kicks a magazine on the floor.)*

ELIZABETH. Is this the lucky one?

(She kicks another magazine and shouts...)

How bout this one? Or maybe this one?

*(**MARILYN** looks towards the bedroom.)*

MARILYN. *(a bit frightened)* Kitty? Katherine? *(louder)* Where are you?

KATHY. (OS) Coming...

*(**ELIZABETH** stops her frenzy and starts to calm down.)*

ELIZABETH. *(deep breath)* I give up.

(She takes a seat, exhausted.)

MARILYN. *(sheepishly)* It wasn't all magazines, honey. I started getting all these emails about investing in property.

*(**ELIZABETH** looks defeated.)*

ELIZABETH. Property? Where?

MARILYN. *(slowly)* In South Africa. It was a gold mine, actually. They sent me pictures and I read all about it. I was promised a 50% return on my investment. At first I just sent them a little bit of money, and they sent me some of the gold they had just mined. I invested a little more and a few months later I received a check and more gold.

ELIZABETH. Don't tell me. You invested it all and never heard from them again.

MARILYN. *(guilty)* Something like that. I tried to contact the authorities, from the police to the government. No one could help me. That was a big loss.

ELIZABETH. So you went back to playing the magazines. How much have you invested in these contests lately?

MARILYN. I don't know, not too much. I don't have that much left. But this contest is legit, honey. And it's the last one I'll ever do.

ELIZABETH. *(frustrated)* Oh, Mom. I don't know what to do with you.

MARILYN. Don't be like that, sweetheart. God is able to redeem what the enemy has stolen from me. When he does, I'll do something for you. When I get my winnings, I'll give you that thousand dollars straight away. How does that sound?

(**ELIZABETH**, *not knowing what to do just shakes her head, and then weakly smiles at her mother.* **MARILYN** *smiles back.*)

ELIZABETH. *(shaken)* I'll go see what's taking Kathy so long.

(**ELIZABETH** *gets up and exits to bedroom.* **MARILYN** *proceeds to pick up all the magazines and put them on the table. There is a soft KNOCK at the door.*)

MARILYN. *(calling)* I'll get it.

(**MARILYN** *goes to the door, opens it a crack and then lets* **EDWARD** *in.*)

EDWARD. Good evening Mrs. Van Pelt.

MARILYN. Hello Edward. Come on in and sit down. The girls will be out in a minute.

EDWARD. Thank you.

(**EDWARD** *puts his briefcase down and sits while* **MARILYN** *straightens up.*)

MARILYN. Can I get you something cold to drink?

EDWARD. I'm fine, thanks. How are you feeling?

MARILYN. Not too bad, considering. How are you?

EDWARD. Just rushed. I have a lot going on right now. But I have to make sure your lovely daughters are taken care of.

MARILYN. Aren't you sweet.

(She runs a hand through her hair.)

EDWARD. *(winking)* And I can see where they get their good looks.

MARILYN. *(smiles)* Oh, stop. I'm just an old lady.

EDWARD. *(playing with her)* No you're not, I'm sure you still turn heads.

(She sits next to him.)

MARILYN. You know, I looked just like Elizabeth at her age. Kitty favors her father.

EDWARD. They are both very special. And try not to worry too much about the case, we have the best people in my office working on it.

MARILYN. Edward, dear. This has been so shocking to realize that my poor Kitty has such severe emotional problems.

EDWARD. *(uncomfortable)* And... Where are they?

*(**MARILYN** motions to the bedroom.)*

MARILYN. But before I go get them, I do want to thank you for all you're doing for us. You must charge a bundle.

EDWARD. Not a problem. I am very fond of Elizabeth and we'll work it out in trade.

MARILYN. *(eyes blinking)* Trade?

EDWARD. *(chuckling)* Bunny, my daughter, takes dance lessons. And I'm taking some too.

MARILYN. *(relieved)* You know I was quite a hoofer in my day. *(flirtatiously)* And I'm sure you're very smooth on the dance floor, too.

EDWARD. Au contraire, I have two left feet. My ex wanted me to learn years ago so we'd be able to go dancing. I refused. Now I'm finally ready to give it a try.

ELIZABETH. *(calling* **OS***)* Ed? Is that you?

EDWARD. *(calling back)* Yes.

ELIZABETH. (OS) Sorry. Be right out!

MARILYN. What steps is Elizabeth teaching you?

EDWARD. Oh, I'm just learning some basic ballroom. It's alright, but to tell you the truth, *(leaning towards her)* I really want to learn how to Tango.

MARILYN. *(horrified)* Oooh, no you don't.

EDWARD. I do. I've watched it on television.

MARILYN. But it's a dirty dance!

EDWARD. Dirty?

MARILYN. I think it comes from Satan!

EDWARD. Who?

MARILYN. Satan! You know, the devil? The underworld?

(EDWARD is stiffly uncomfortable. ELIZABETH enters and he pops up.)

ELIZABETH. Kathy will be out in a minute. She doesn't feel well.

EDWARD. Hi Elizabeth.

(ELIZABETH walks over to him and gives him a hug.)

ELIZABETH. Hi. I'm so glad you're here.

(He is pleased.)

ELIZABETH. Looks like you've had a chance to have another nice chat with my mother.

(They smile at each other. His phone rings and he looks at it.)

EDWARD. Sorry, got to take this.

(He walks away and talks on his cell.)

KATHY enters holding a folder.)

KATHY. Biz, I need the phone again. I forgot to give Tony this. They'll need it for the concert.

ELIZABETH. Can't I just fax it to him?

KATHY. No, he needs this whole thing.

(holding it up)

I've written notes on the back of the folder, too. I'll call him and see if he can pick it up tomorrow. After school, when we get back.

ELIZABETH. Alright. But wait till Edward leaves.

(KATHY looks at her mother questioningly. ELIZABETH hands her the cell phone.)

KATHY. Mom? Why are you here?

MARILYN. To help you Kitty. Where else should I be?

(**EDWARD** *puts his phone away and approaches.*)

EDWARD. Hello Kathy. How are you holding up?

KATHY. I'm glad to be home.

EDWARD. Good. There are things we will need to go over, but I don't have much time now, something's come up. I will act as your attorney for the hearing tomorrow.

ELIZABETH. We owe you so much, Edward, thank you.

EDWARD. I have to cut this very short. But I did hear that Sal's parents don't want a big spectacle. They are worried about his mental health.

ELIZABETH. What does that mean for us?

EDWARD. It's a good thing. Kathy will be charged but we may be able to plead out.

KATHY. Do I have to do anything tomorrow?

EDWARD. No. I'll do the talking. It will be very simple. You will just be asked to enter a plea to the charges that are read. And you will say not guilty.

KATHY. Not guilty?

EDWARD. (*composing himself*) Let's all sit for a moment.

(*They sit.*)

EDWARD. First, you are not guilty of all the charges, I'm sure. What I'm advising you to do is very common. And, you do have some emotional issues that are not your fault.

MARILYN. Are you going to tell them that Kitty's crazy?

ELIZABETH. Mom, please be quiet and let Edward do his work.

EDWARD. Your daughter is not crazy, Mrs. Van Pelt. Perhaps she wasn't able to determine right from wrong at the time but I wouldn't call that "crazy."

KATHY. But I did know that what I was doing was technically wrong.

MARILYN. Quiet!

EDWARD. Kathy, let's not get into that now. Please trust me. (*carefully*) All you have to do tomorrow is appear before the judge and say not guilty and I am certain we will be able to enter into a plea bargain. Sal's parents don't want this turned into a circus any more than you or I do. In fact, I heard his father wants to drop everything.

KATHY. Will I be able to teach again?

(**EDWARD** *ignores and rises.*)

EDWARD. I need to get back to my office. Elizabeth? Can you and Kathy come a little early tomorrow morning? We can meet and go over this again.

ELIZABETH. Yes. We can be there an hour early. Should we wait for you in front of the courthouse?

EDWARD. No. There's a coffee shop across the street, you can't miss it. Let's meet there and review all this. Much better to talk then, I'm too rushed now. I'll call you later.

ELIZABETH. Thanks Ed. I'll walk you out.

MARILYN. Goodbye Mr. Green.

(*They all stand,* **EDWARD** *turns and hastily waves. He and* **ELIZABETH** *exit.*)

MARILYN. (*to* **KATHY**) He's a nice man, isn't he?

KATHY. Yes, he's nice I suppose.

MARILYN. And obviously mad about Elizabeth, do you think she likes him?

KATHY. As a friend.

MARILYN. (*frustrated*) I wonder why she doesn't grab him up.

KATHY. She said he's boring.

MARILYN. Boring? What's the matter with her? He's attractive, and he makes a good living. What more could she want?

KATHY. To be in love, I suppose.

MARILYN. Don't be childish. At her age she needs to find an appropriate partner. And she better hurry, I'm almost giving up. You know how much I want grandchildren.

KATHY. I know.

MARILYN. Now I'm sure you're scared about tomorrow but

just do everything Edward says to do.

KATHY. It will be hard to say I'm not guilty if they ask me about our relationship.

MARILYN. *(shaking her head)* Even if you think you're guilty, you need not feel guilty. The Lord has made provisions for our sins. Even the worst of them, to be forgiven.

KATHY. Momma, you don't understand.

MARILYN. Be strong, Kitty. I'll get us some orange soda.

(**MARILYN** *gets up and goes to get two glasses and faces* **KATHY**.)

MARILYN. *(dramatically)* It's time to start the healing. Our Lord paid the penalty for your sins and you have to ask Him to forgive you. And He wants to, because he loves you.

(**ELIZABETH** *comes back into the house and approaches them.*)

MARILYN. Your part is to believe with all your heart.

ELIZABETH. What am I interrupting, a holy powwow?

MARILYN. Don't be flip. The unrighteous will not inherit the kingdom of God.

ELIZABETH. *(throwing her hands up)* Sorry. I'm tired, upset, and we need to be practical. Kathy, we have a few things to go over that Edward suggested.

MARILYN. Do everything Edward says. You will confess and cleanse later.

ELIZABETH. I need to run home and pick up some clothes. I'm gonna sleep here tonight.

KATHY. Why, do you consider me a flight risk?

ELIZABETH. No, that's not it. It would just be less stressful, for me, if I didn't have to rush and pick you up so early, that's all.

MARILYN. That's very generous of you, Elizabeth. You know, that Edward fella is quite a nice man. He has children, doesn't he?

ELIZABETH. Yes, ten year old twins – Bunny and Jerrod.

MARILYN. *(musing)* I wonder if he would want more children.

Assuming he met the right woman, of course.

ELIZABETH. Don't start up with that again. You know I don't want kids.

MARILYN. I hate when you say that. I pray for you to come to your senses. "Children are a blessing from the Lord – Happy is the man who has a passel of them."

KATHY. Maybe I'll have children.

(**MARILYN** *completely ignores* **KATHY**.)

MARILYN. *(to* **ELIZABETH***)* I don't know what you have against settling down, Elizabeth. And having a proper family. I just don't know what's wrong with you.

KATHY. I'm feeling sick.

ELIZABETH. So am I.

MARILYN. It's just nerves. I'll get us that orange soda.

(**MARILYN** *gets up and pulls out the orange soda.*)

KATHY. Momma, would you love my children, too?

(**MARILYN** *turns around.*)

MARILYN. Of course, I would love your children, Kitty.

(to **ELIZABETH***)*

Do you enjoy teaching Edward dance lessons?

ELIZABETH. Sure, it's fun. I don't teach much anymore.

(**MARILYN** *gets some glasses and starts pouring.*)

MARILYN. Some words of wisdom. Sometimes it takes time to fall in love.

ELIZABETH. That's it, Mom. This conversation is closed.

KATHY. Did you like being pregnant, Mom?

MARILYN. Oh yes, I loved everything about that miracle.

KATHY. Did you get morning sickness?

MARILYN. Just in the beginning.

KATHY. Were you tired, too?

(**ELIZABETH** *has stopped what she's doing and is staring at* **KATHY**. **MARILYN** *brings two glasses of soda to the girls.*)

MARILYN. *(nonchalantly)* More at the end of the pregnancies.

I felt pretty good after that nauseous feeling left. Here.

(**KATHY** *takes the glass.* **ELIZABETH** *is frozen and ignores her. A moment.*)

ELIZABETH. What's with all these questions?

MARILYN. *(dismissing her thoughts)* You should listen, honey, maybe you'll learn something. Here girls, take your soda.

(**ELIZABETH** *takes it and puts it down.*)

ELIZABETH. Kathy?

(**KATHY** *doesn't answer.* **MARILYN** *sits.*)

ELIZABETH. Kathy? You don't think you're pregnant, do you?

MARILYN. That's ridiculous.

(**MARILYN** *turns to* **KATHY**.)

MARILYN. Isn't it?

(**KATHY** *still doesn't answer and* **ELIZABETH** *looks ready to faint.*)

MARILYN. Isn't it? *(sternly)* Katherine! Don't even kid around about something like that.

KATHY. I thought you wanted a grandchild.

ELIZABETH. Oh, no. Please, no.

(**ELIZABETH** *collapses on sofa in a heap.*)

KATHY. *(proudly shakes her head yes)* Confirmed by a pregnancy kit from the drug store.

(**MARILYN** *looks at* **ELIZABETH** *and then stares at* **KATHY** *in disbelief. She rises.*)

MARILYN. *(pleasantly)* Oh. I forgot to pour myself some orange soda.

(*Another moment.*)

ELIZABETH. Stop it, Mom. Don't block that out, I know you heard it. *(with emphasis)* Yes! Kathy is pregnant.

(**MARILYN** *stops and covers her mouth and lets out a*

moan. **KATHY** *is confused.*)

ELIZABETH. Alright, let's not panic. It's early.

KATHY. Yes, I just started getting morning sickness.

(**MARILYN** *is shaken.*)

ELIZABETH. And I have a great doctor, he'll take care of everything. We'll go see him next week.

KATHY. I want to see him soon. I want to talk to him before I tell Sal.

(**MARILYN** *covers her ears.*)

MARILYN. *(screaming)* Stop it, you silly girl! What have you done?

(*Hurt,* **KATHY** *looks at* **ELIZABETH.** **ELIZABETH** *puts her arm around her.*)

ELIZABETH. You can't have this baby, Kitty. You know that.

(**KATHY** *tears herself away.*)

KATHY. *(furious)* What are you suggesting?

(*She looks at* **ELIZABETH**, *then her mother, who shaking her head.*)

KATHY. Mom?

MARILYN. You silly, silly girl.

KATHY. Did you hear what Biz is saying?

MARILYN. *(stammering)* Yes. And. And…I…

KATHY. You what?

(A moment.)

MARILYN. *(troubled)* Oh, what have you done?

KATHY. But Mom? Did you hear what Biz wants me to do?

MARILYN. *(pause)* Yes, Katherine. And of course you can't have that baby.

KATHY. *(shocked)* Am I hearing you correctly. After all your lectures?

MARILYN. You are to go with Elizabeth. To her doctor.

KATHY. *(shocked)* How can you say that! You, of all people!

MARILYN. Your life would be ruined. And so would that

young boy's.

KATHY. How about the bible, Momma. *(softly)* "When I was growing there in secret, You knew I was there. You saw me before I was born."

(**ELIZABETH** *sits down and puts her hands over her ears.* **MARILYN** *points at* **KATHY** *threateningly.*)

MARILYN. Don't you quote the good book to me.

KATHY. "My frame was not hidden from You, when I was made in secret, And skillfully wrought in the lowest parts of the earth."

(**MARILYN** *looks away.* **KATHY** *approaches her.*)

KATHY. *(to* **MARILYN***)* "Your eyes saw my substance, being yet unformed. And in Your book they all were written, The days fashioned for me when as yet there were none of them...'"

(*No response.* **MARILYN** *sits.*)

KATHY. You want me to have an abortion? You... who call it murder?

MARILYN. This is different, Katherine. I'm sorry.

KATHY. Why is this different? You want me to kill my baby? Your grandchild?

(**MARILYN** *gets up and cannot face* **KATHY**.)

MARILYN. *(softly)* You will go to the doctor with your sister.

KATHY. *(angry)* You used to say that you can't pick and choose when you want to follow HIS teachings.

MARILYN. This is a special case.

KATHY. *(loudly)* No it's not. You're a hypocrite, a big fraud!

MARILYN. Enough, Katherine. Don't talk to me that way. It's a sin.

KATHY. *(interrupting)* You think I'm a sinner and you're so virtuous? You're not supposed to use prayer for selfish reasons. Well, I know that you pray every day to win one of your stupid contests. Is that so righteous, o noble mother?

MARILYN. Stop it, Katherine.

KATHY. *(shouting)* I will not stop it. You are a holy phony! And you told us you wanted a grandchild.

MARILYN. Not like this.

KATHY. Because you only want Elizabeth to have a child. Why don't you want MY grandchild, Momma. Do you hate me that much?

ELIZABETH. *(standing up)* Kitty, that's ridiculous. Mom loves both of us.

KATHY. No she doesn't and you know it! She hates me. I'm just like Daddy.

ELIZABETH. *(pleading)* Tell her she's wrong, Mom.

KATHY. Yes, my pious mother. Tell me I'm wrong and then prove you're a liar, too. Come on, Momma, look me in the eyes and tell me you love me as much as Elizabeth.

(**KATHY** *walks right up to her and faces her.*)

KATHY. But first, let me remind you about Proverbs. The six things which the Lord hates? One of them is a "lying tongue," remember? So go on... Tell me you love us both the same. Do it, I dare you. Sin a little more in the eyes of your Lord.

(**MARILYN** *looks down defeated.* **KATHY** *waits.* **MARILYN** *slowly turns away.*)

MARILYN. I'm leaving.

ELIZABETH. *(shocked)* Aren't you going to answer Kathy?

MARILYN. I won't be talked to like that.

ELIZABETH. *(raising her voice)* Mom, tell Kathy she's wrong.

(**MARILYN** *gets her purse and turns away.*)

ELIZABETH. *(furious)* Fine. This is great! *(gesturing)* Then just get the hell out of here. You should be happy at least one of your daughters can be in love.

(**MARILYN** *heads towards the door, hanging her head.*)

KATHY. *(sheepishly)* Momma?

(**MARILYN** *slowly turns around.*)

KATHY. *(softly)* You can lie if you want to...

(**MARILYN** *looks at the girls, takes a moment, looks at the ground, turns and exits – a confused woman.* **KATHY** *softly cries.*

ELIZABETH *turns to* **KATHY** *and gives her a hug. She helps her to the sofa.*)

ELIZABETH. She's just saying crazy stuff, you know she loves you.

(**ELIZABETH** *sits down beside her. She puts her arms around her to try to comfort her.*

KATHY *stares at the floor, not moving. A moment.*)

ELIZABETH. Of course she does. Now let's get you into bed, you must be exhausted. And I better go get my stuff before it gets too late.

(gets up)

Why don't you watch TV til I get back.

(*She sticks out her hand and pulls* **KATHY** *up who's in a daze.*)

ELIZABETH. And we'll take one thing at a time, you don't have to make any decisions now... about anything. Except what you're going to wear tomorrow. Come on.

(*She puts her arms around* **KATHY**, *whose head is down, and assists her to the bedroom.*)

ELIZABETH. I love you, Kitty, you know that. And I'll always be there for you.

(*They exit to the bedroom and* **ELIZABETH** *reenters, grabs her purse and heads towards the door.*)

KATHY. (OS) When are you coming back?

ELIZABETH. In about an hour, or so. Will you be alright?

KATHY. (OS) I'll be in bed, I'll probably just go to sleep.

ELIZABETH. That's fine. Why don't you leave a key under

the mat and I'll let myself in.

(She opens the door, stops, turns and calls out.)

ELIZABETH. Okay?

KATHY. (OS) Okay. I'll do that right now. *(a moment)* And take your time, I'll be fine.

ELIZABETH. I'll be back soon. Bye.

*(**ELIZABETH** leaves and closes the door behind her. Silence on stage.*

*A moment later **KATHY** appears with a jacket on. She grabs her purse, puts a key under the mat, and rushes out the door.)*

(BLACKOUT.)

Scene 2

(SEVERAL HOURS LATER.

A frantic classical piano piece is POUNDING while the stage is dark.

A fumbling with the door lock is heard. The music stops as **KATHY** *opens the door, enters her apartment and turns on the light...*

To find an angry, tired **ELIZABETH**, *in pajamas with her coat on, laying on the sofa waiting for her.)*

KATHY. *(screams)* Ah! You scared me!

ELIZABETH. *(sternly)* No, you scared me. Where have you been?

KATHY. *(fumbling)* I got hungry...and then I figured I'd do an errand –

(**ELIZABETH** *gets up and grabs her.)*

ELIZABETH. Did you see Sal?

(**KATHY** *faces her but doesn't answer.)*

ELIZABETH. *(shouting)* I told you to stay away from him! You're in big trouble! What's the matter with you!

(**KATHY** *pushes her away and steps back.)*

KATHY. *(defiantly)* Leave me alone, I'm very upset!

ELIZABETH. You're upset?

(She sits down and stares at the floor. **ELIZABETH** *fumes.)*

KATHY. *(bursting)* He doesn't want to see me anymore.

(**KATHY** *starts crying.* **ELIZABETH** *doesn't know what to do but sits down next to her.)*

KATHY. *(crazed)* I shouldn't have told him about the baby. He wasn't ready.

ELIZABETH. Oh God. What did he say?

KATHY. He got upset. He started crying. I shouldn't have said anything with all this confusion.

ELIZABETH. Kathy, listen to me and calm down. We're all confused right now.

KATHY. *(in denial)* I don't understand why he said that.

ELIZABETH. *(calmly)* Don't try to understand anything right now. We'll figure it out later. We just have to get through tomorrow, your future is at stake.

(gets up)

Now let's try to relax and get a decent night sleep. We'll figure out everything else later. Please, Kathy.

KATHY. *(muttering)* I don't understand.

ELIZABETH. Come on.

(Elizabeth pulls a DVD out of her purse.)

ELIZABETH. Look.

(holds it up)

I brought over a film. "A League of their Own."

KATHY. I don't want to watch a movie right now.

ELIZABETH. *(coaxing)* Come on, Biz. I want to. It's our favorite. How many times have we seen it?

KATHY. *(looking up)* I don't know. Lots.

ELIZABETH. *(calmly)* Let's watch it – it'll make us happy.

*(**ELIZABETH**, smiles, wiggles the film and motions towards the bedroom.)*

ELIZABETH. You'll change and we'll get into bed. Just like the old times. Come on. There's no crying in baseball...

*(Slowly **KATHY** gets up. **ELIZABETH** guides her into the bedroom.)*

(SLOW FADE OUT.)

SCENE 3

*(**THE NEXT DAY**.*

The afternoon after the hearing.

Lights up on an empty stage and a loud KNOCK. Another KNOCK and then a key jiggles the front door lock.

*The door opens slowly and **MARILYN**, carrying a plate, and her purse, steps inside tentatively, looking around.)*

MARILYN. Hello? Anybody home?

(She enters and places the plate of cookies on the table and looks around.

She opens her purse, takes out a candle and a vial. She lights the candle. She then turns, stands in the middle of the apartment, and unscrews the little bottle which is filled with scented oil.

She dabs her finger with oil and starts to walk around the apartment, touching the walls and doorways with her finger.)

MARILYN. I anoint this place in the name of Jesus. Let this be a sweet smelling aroma to You.

(She dips her finger again with oil and starts touching the furniture in silent prayer.

She continues this process and mutters to herself occasionally looking upwards.

After walking around the apartment, she finishes, puts the bottle of oil on the counter and clasps her hands in prayer.)

MARILYN. *(slowly)* Holy Spirit, I pray You will heal whatever is in my daughter's body that needs Your healing.

(A moment, she caps the vial and puts it back in her purse.

She then walks over to the candle and faces it.)

MARILYN. *(painfully)* And dear God, forgive me. Please give me understanding in my heart for Katherine. Help me to be Jesus to her, to love her and accept her as You do.

(She closes her eyes and bows her head. Voices are heard offstage – coming towards to door. **MARILYN** *hears them, is startled, blows out the candle, and clearly isn't sure what to. She freezes as the door opens.*

KATHY, *holds the door open as* **ELIZABETH** *and* **EDWARD** *enter talking.*

MARILYN *confidently comes forward cheerfully.)*

MARILYN. *(smiling)* Hello. My, everyone looks so nice today.

(They are all startled. **KATHY**, *with her head down, exits briskly to the bedroom.)*

ELIZABETH. *(stunned)* Mom? What are you doing here?

MARILYN. Cookies. I made some cookies.

*(***ELIZABETH*** and ***EDWARD*** just stare at her.)*

ELIZABETH. But –

MARILYN. *(interrupting)* I have my own key, you know that. And I know you had some official business this morning so I wanted to bring over something cheerful. Go ahead, Edward, have one.

*(***ELIZABETH*** puts her purse down.* ***EDWARD*** *looks at the plate.)*

EDWARD. That was very thoughtful.

MARILYN. I put sprinkles on them. Just the way Kathy likes them.

ELIZABETH. Everything went well today. Edward did great, Mom.

MARILYN. Oh, thank you Edward. I knew you were a blessing.

EDWARD. I didn't have to do much. I just reminded them how hard a trial would be on Sal.

MARILYN. Honey, please go and tell Kathy I made her favorite cookies.

(**ELIZABETH** *goes to the bedroom.*)

EDWARD. Is something burning?

MARILYN. No, don't worry, I lit a special candle. It was a signal flare to the heavens.

EDWARD. I see.

MARILYN. You are probably smelling the anointing oil, too. That lets the Angels know that we need special attention during this time.

(**ELIZABETH** *comes back into the living room,* **EDWARD** *looks relieved.*)

ELIZABETH. Mom, Kathy's not coming out. And she said she doesn't like those cookies anymore.

MARILYN. No? Those were her very favorite.

ELIZABETH. You better go, Mom. Everything's going to be alright.

(**MARILYN** *thinks about it and then looks at her watch.*)

MARILYN. Oh, I have to skedaddle. I have a very important appointment but I wanted to come here first.

(*She gets her purse and prepares to leave.*)

MARILYN. Keep me posted?

ELIZABETH. Sure, Mom.

MARILYN. Nice seeing you, honey. And Edward, I do so hope to see you again.

EDWARD. It's been a pleasure.

(**MARILYN** *looks toward the bedroom and shouts.*)

MARILYN. *(loudly)* Bye Kitty.

(*No response. She turns and opens the front door.* **ELIZABETH** *comes with her.*)

MARILYN. *(to Elizabeth)* I guess I should have brought chocolate chip brownies.

ELIZABETH. It's fine, Mom. Goodbye.

(**ELIZABETH** *closes the door. She looks back at* **EDWARD**.)

ELIZABETH. Please, don't say anything. Just have a cookie.

(**ELIZABETH** *sits back down on the sofa.* **EDWARD** *walks over and takes a cookie.*)

ELIZABETH. *(softly)* Would you like to stay a few minutes?

EDWARD. I could. I don't have any meetings scheduled.

(**ELIZABETH** *rises and walks towards him.*)

ELIZABETH. Please stay. And let me take your jacket.

EDWARD. Not necessary. I could just...

(**EDWARD** *starts to take off his suit jacket.* **ELIZABETH** *puts her arms on his shoulders and helps him, slowly, peel it off. A moment of chemistry as they touch.* **ELIZABETH** *holds his jacket.*)

EDWARD. I've been meaning to tell you, Liz. I want to learn how to do the Tango.

ELIZABETH. The Tango? Why?

EDWARD. It's inspiring. It looks like a dance for someone who wants to understand what it takes to be a pleasure to dance with.

(**ELIZABETH** *turns away and busies herself putting his jacket neatly over the chair.*)

ELIZABETH. *(a bit shyly)* To tell you the truth, Ed, I haven't tangoed in a long time. You can take from Diana. She knows the moves.

EDWARD. I don't want to take from her. I'd be uncomfortable.

(*She turns and faces him.*)

ELIZABETH. *(considering)* Alright, but I just remember the basics. I'll have to brush up on the complicated steps.

EDWARD. Even better. We can figure it out together.

(*They look at each other. A loud KNOCK at the door.* **ELIZABETH** *jumps up and yells to* **KATHY**.)

ELIZABETH. Kathy? Are you expecting anyone?

(**KATHY** *shouts from the bedroom.*)

KATHY. (OS) It's Tony. To pick up that music folder.

(**EDWARD** *is visibly disappointed.* **ELIZABETH**, *not particularly happy, gets up and swings open the door.*)

ELIZABETH. Hello Tony, come on in.

TONY. Hi. Sorry to bother you.

ELIZABETH. (*fake smile*) No bother.

(*He sees* **EDWARD**.)

TONY. Hey, counselor.

(**EDWARD** *nods.* **KATHY** *comes out with a folder in her hand. It is obvious she has been crying.*)

KATHY. (*looking down*) Here's the finale, sorry bout that. I thought everything was in one place.

TONY. No big deal. I wanted to check on you anyway. Is everything okay?

(**KATHY** *shakes her head "no" and hands* **TONY** *the folder.*)

ELIZABETH. Kathy should be happy, considering there won't be a trial.

TONY. You're kidding?

EDWARD. No, we're very pleased. Two years probation with psychological counseling.

TONY. That's all?

EDWARD. Yes. Sal's parents didn't want to subject him to court, it's over. Kathy does have to give up her teaching credential, though.

ELIZABETH. But she can teach private piano lessons. And I have plans for Kathy at my studio when she's ready.

(**KATHY** *sits down, pouting, while they are talking about her like she's invisible.*)

TONY. (*surprised*) You mean she can still teach kids?

EDWARD. She wasn't labeled a sex offender, Tony. No

witness stepped forward, nothing was proven. You have a problem with that?

TONY. *(quickly)* Of course not, I was just asking.

(**KATHY** *turns away.*)

EDWARD. The judge sees it like I do. She's not a sexual predator. If anything happened it was a one time thing. And counseling, *(lowering his voice)* A little therapy, will help.

TONY. They think that's going to help?

EDWARD. Yes, don't you?

KATHY. I don't need therapy.

TONY. And how bout Sal? What does Sal get?

EDWARD. He'll be with his parents, Tony. They'll decide what's best for him. He'll probably get some counseling, too.

TONY. That won't do anything.

KATHY. Tony's right, we don't need counseling. I can't stand this conversation. In fact, Tony's the only person I want to talk to right now.

ELIZABETH. That's gratitude after all I've done for you.

(**KATHY** *faces her.*)

KATHY. Done for me? Hardly! This was all about you. Me not embarrassing you.

ELIZABETH. *(surprised)* What are you talking about?

KATHY. *(defiantly)* You don't care how I feel. Tony is the only person here who cares about my feelings.

ELIZABETH. *(cautioning)* Now you're making me really mad.

KATHY. It's true. You just want this "incident" to go away for your own sake. Your reputation. I trust Tony, he doesn't have an agenda like you both do.

(**ELIZABETH** *shakes her head in disgust.* **EDWARD** *looks at* **ELIZABETH** *and then* **KATHY**.)

EDWARD. You really feel that way, Kathy?

KATHY. Yes. In fact you can both leave right now. We don't need you anymore.

TONY. *(awkwardly)* Kathy, I better go.

(**KATHY** *goes to the refrigerator and gets a beer.*)

KATHY. No, Tony, please sit down. I want you here. At least you understand. And you're on my side.

EDWARD. Yes, Tony, please sit down. It seems you're the only one here on Kathy's side.

(**ELIZABETH** *looks at* **EDWARD** *questioningly.* **KATHY** *hands* **TONY** *a beer.*)

KATHY. Biz, you never even tried to understand.

(**KATHY** *sits next to* **TONY**. **ELIZABETH** *rises.*)

ELIZABETH. If you feel that way, then I'll leave.

EDWARD. *(to* **KATHY***)* Alright, we'll go so Kathy can be with Tony. Someone she trusts.

(**ELIZABETH** *rises.* **EDWARD** *gets up and starts putting on his jacket.*)

EDWARD. Tony? Let me ask you something before we leave.

TONY. Sure.

(**TONY** *drinks some beer.*)

EDWARD. Kathy just said you're the only person who cares about her.

TONY. Uh, huh.

EDWARD. Is that why you called Sal's mother and told on them?

TONY. *(stunned)* What?

(**KATHY** *whirls around and looks at him. He puts the beer down.*)

EDWARD. I know you were the witness, Tony.

TONY. What are you talking about?

EDWARD. You blew the whistle on their relationship. And even though the charges were dropped, the prosecutor might have continued the case but you wouldn't testify.

TONY. *(shaking his head)* It wasn't me. I didn't know anything.

KATHY. That's right, Tony didn't know.

EDWARD. You were specifically named in Sal's mother's statement.

(**KATHY** *gets up.*)

TONY. *(flustered)* Well, maybe it was me.

(**TONY** *stands up and faces* **KATHY**. **ELIZABETH** *and* **EDWARD** *freeze.*)

TONY. Okay. I saw you guys leave school last week. And I followed you.

KATHY. *(stunned)* And called Sal's mother?

(*A silence, nobody moves.*)

KATHY. Tony, we were friends.

TONY. Sorry, but I had to do something.

KATHY. Why?

(**TONY** *looks down.*)

KATHY. *(getting increasingly angry)* Why?

(*approaches him*)

When I stuck up for you last year at the faculty meeting you said you'd always be there for me.

TONY. I know. But this is different.

(**TONY** *walks away.*)

TONY. I was worried.

KATHY. *(incredulous)* About what?

TONY. Sal. You're gonna hurt him, Kathy.

KATHY. I'd never hurt him. I love him!

(**TONY** *gets his backpack and turns to leave.*)

KATHY. You were my friend, my best friend!

(*He turns and faces her.*)

TONY. I better go.

(**KATHY** *confronts him.*)

KATHY. I don't understand!

TONY. You wouldn't.

KATHY. You're a liar! And a terrible person!

(*He turns away. She is furious. He starts to head for the door.*)

KATHY. And ya know what? You're a mediocre artist... at best. And a pathetic excuse for a musician.

(**TONY** *stops.*)

KATHY. You can't even keep time!

TONY. (*turning to her*) You don't have a clue, do you.

KATHY. About what?

TONY. About the damage you may be causing.

KATHY. (*incredulous*) To Sal? We're in love!

(*He comes back into the room determined, and approaches her.*)

TONY. He's a child, Kathy. And he can't handle these emotions yet.

KATHY. You're the one who can't handle emotions. And I thought you understood.

TONY. That's the problem. I do understand.

KATHY. No you don't!

TONY. Yes I do.

(**EDWARD** *steps forward.*)

EDWARD. Why did you leave your last job, Tony?

TONY. What?

EDWARD. Tony, I know you were fired from your last teaching position. Remember, I'm a lawyer. I did some checking.

TONY. So? I didn't get along with the administration. That's all.

EDWARD. And the school before that?

TONY. I quit. I felt stifled there. You won't find any dirt on me.

EDWARD. No? Why were you really protecting Sal?

TONY. *(getting angry)* I told you. Sal's a wonderful boy. And I was worried that he'd get screwed up.

EDWARD. Or were you jealous of Kathy's relationship with him.

TONY. Nothing like that!

EDWARD. Were you attracted to Sal, Tony?

TONY. No! Fuck off!

KATHY. *(covering her ears)* I thought I knew you. But you're crazy!

TONY. *(shouting back)* Fine. I may be crazy, Kathy. *(exploding)* But somebody like you made me that way.

(Confusion. Silence.)

Yeah.

(Everybody waits for him to speak.)

TONY. I was 10 years old. *(deep breath)* And I had this baby sitter.

*(**TONY** closes his eyes and clenches his fists. He takes a moment.)*

TONY. A teenager. She went to the local high school.

*(**TONY** slowly sits down and opens his eyes.)*

Well, I was a real active little boy. And I never wanted to go to sleep. My baby sitter wanted me out of the picture so she could watch her TV shows and talk on the phone. So she figured something out.

(embarrassed)

We'd go into my bedroom and she'd get under the covers with me.

(A moment.)

And we had a routine. She was dressed, but I wasn't.

(with difficulty)

She said it was to make me relax and have good dreams. And it worked. She'd read me a book, something stupid, and then...

(closing his eyes)

Well, then, she'd touch me. Just straight masturbation. And I'd settle down and go to sleep. This went on for a coupla years.

(**KATHY** *sits, not facing him. Not wanting to listen, puts her head between her legs.*)

ELIZABETH. *(stunned)* How old was she?

TONY. Eighteen when I met her. She stopped coming over when I turned twelve and my parents thought I could stay home by myself.

(a moment)

It screwed me up. When I got older, it ruined my relationships.

(*He stands up and faces them. He is holding back tears.*)

TONY. I had weird thoughts. And how long would a woman put up with a guy who loved to just lie there every night and have someone masturbate him to sleep.

(**TONY** *tries to gather himself.*)

TONY. Friends said I was a lucky, but I wasn't lucky. It was what they call abuse, and I suffered some real psychological damage.

(*He turns to* **EDWARD**.)

TONY. And I had therapy and "counseling." I could even intellectualize everything, but it didn't help. It didn't change my feelings.

(**EDWARD** *gets up and walks towards him.*)

EDWARD. I apologize, Tony. I was wrong. And I'm sorry.

(**EDWARD** *looks at* **ELIZABETH** *and* **KATHY**.)

EDWARD. Your secret is safe with us.

(**EDWARD** *shakes Tony's hand.* **TONY** *is ashamed and looks away.*)

TONY. *(sniffs)* Sal's a sweet boy, Kathy. I really like you. You were my friend, and I know your intentions are pure. But I didn't want him to have his demons later on.

(There is a silent moment. **KATHY** *looks up at him and shakes her head.)*

KATHY. *(coldly)* This is completely different.

(gets up)

But it doesn't matter anyway. Thanks to you, Sal doesn't want to have anything to do with me anymore.

ELIZABETH. I'm very sorry, Tony. I don't know what to say...

TONY. *(interrupting)* Yeah, I'm sorry too. That this whole thing had to happen.

*(***TONY*** *heads for the door. He opens it, turns, doesn't know what else to say...and exits.*

EDWARD *and* ***ELIZABETH*** *just watch him go. A moment passes. They finally look at each other.*

KATHY *stands up.)*

KATHY. And I want you both to leave, too.

ELIZABETH. *(dismissive)* Kitty, forget about him. He was a nice guy but had some strange –

KATHY. *(interrupting)* Get out!

*(***ELIZABETH*** *is stunned and rises. She approaches* ***KATHY*** *and starts to reach for her arm.)*

ELIZABETH. *(earnestly)* Kitty, I'm just trying to help...

*(***KATHY*** *shakes her off.)*

KATHY. *(coldly)* Get out!

(They lock eyes for a moment. ***ELIZABETH*** *can't hold the stare, looks down, backs up and puts her hands up.)*

ELIZABETH. *(meekly)* Okay.

*(***EDWARD*** *grabs Elizabeth's purse and approaches her.)*

ELIZABETH. *(confused)* We'll leave.

*(***EDWARD*** *slowly guides her to the door. They exit.*

KATHY *watches them go and wipes away her tears.*

She then turns, and looks around her apartment for a moment. She walks over to two plants and feels their soil for moisture.

Satisfied, she heads to the kitchen where a calendar is hanging on a hook. She looks at it, takes it off the hook, and carries it to the sofa. She sits, and flips the pages ahead, counting months. Piano music begins – simple exercises.

The light slowly narrows and then pinpoints, just on Kathy's face.

She puts the calendar on her lap and looks up, with determination. A few moments, then lights fade out completely.)

END OF PLAY

PROPERTY PLOT

ACT 1 PRESET KATHY'S APARTMENT

FURNITURE:
couch & pillow
end table
magazine racks
floor plants
small kitchen table with two chairs
refrigerator, kitchen counter
bookshelf
plant stand
large kitchen calendar hanging on wall
hanging mirror
prints on walls relating to music and/or flowers
small trash can

HAND PROPS:
On end table:
cordless phone
stacks of magazines
In magazine rack:
more magazes – including "Ebony," " "Bon Apetite," "Field and Stream," "Bowhunting"
books and knick knacks in bookcase
4 glasses
5 bottles of beer in refrigerator
1 large bottle of orange soda
can opener

PERSONAL PROPS:
KATHY:
watering can
small gardening rake
ELIZABETH:
purse
cell phone/blackberry
TONY:
cardboard box
girls jacket
folded piece of paper

EDWARD:
watch
cell phone
wallet
business cards
briefcase
notepad & pen
handkerchief or tissue
MARILYN:
large purse
vial of pills (in purse)
big bangle jewelry, necklaces

ACT TWO
Scene One

Kathy's Apartment
Kathy's Apartment is preset the same as in Act One except the cell phone is not on the table.

PERSONAL PROPS:
KATHY:
notebook/folder
house key
purse
jacket
TONY:
backpack
ELIZABETH:
purse
blackberry/cell phone
Kathy's cell phone
MARILYN: purse
Shopping bag – full of magazines
EDWARD:
briefcase
cell phone

Scene 2
ELIZABETH: DVD – "A League of Their Own"

Scene 3
MARILYN:
Purse
candle
anointing oil
matches
plate of cookies

KATHY:
Notebook/folder
ELIZABETH:
Purse
TONY: Backpack

COSTUME PLOT

ACT ONE

KATHY: Short sleeved, small floral print blouse – round collar, short shirt, barefoot
Black slacks, pink shirt, pumps, and long necklaces
ELIZABETH: Sexy business suit, high heels, coat
TONY: Long sleeved button down shirt, rolled up sleeves, vest, khaki pants, sneakers.
EDWARD: Dark suit, light shirt, conservative tie, dress shoes
MARILYN: Tight leggings, boots, loud colorful blouse, wide belt, muffler, sunglasses, loud costume jewelry

ACT TWO
Scene One:

KATHY:
Pink robe and slippers
Jeans, t-shirt, sandals, jacket
TONY: Polo shirt, slacks, painter beret, sneakers
ELIZABETH: Black stylish dress, high heels, wrap
MARILYN: Garish capris, low cut blouse, too many necklaces, boa, high heels
EDWARD: Suit, conservative tie, dress shoes

Scene Two:
KATHY: Same as scene one
ELIZABETH: Same as scene one
Pajamas, coat

Scene Three:
KATHY: Skirt, blouse, heels, jacket
Jeans, sweatshirt, flip-flops
TONY: Button down shirt, jeans, tie, sneakers
ELIZABETH: Stylish dark business suit, heels
MARILYN: Colorful pattern polyester pant suit, scarf, high platform sandals, cross around neck
EDWARD: Suit, colorful tie, dress shoes

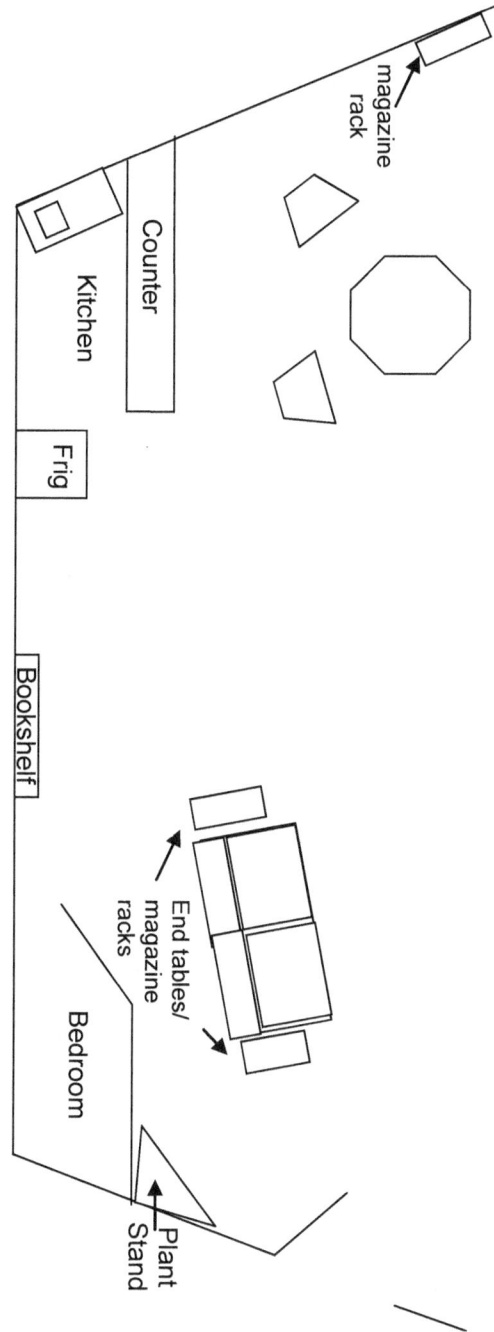

DORIS TO DARLENE
Jordan Harrison

Comedy / 4m, 2f / Unit Set

Doris to Darlene, A Cautionary Valentine: In the candy-colored 1960s, biracial schoolgirl Doris is molded into pop star Darlene by a whiz-kid record producer who culls a top-ten hit out of Richard Wagner's "Liebestod." Rewind to the candy-colored 1860s, where Wagner is writing the melody that will become Darlene's hit song. Fast-forward to the not-so-candy-colored present, where a teenager obsesses over Darlene's music – and his music teacher. Three dissonant decades merge into an unlikely harmony in this time-jumping pop fairy tale about the dreams and disasters behind one transcendent song.

"*Doris to Darlene: A Cautionary Valentine*, at Playwrights Horizons, is a quirky and enjoyable love letter to music and its seductive power to make us lose ourselves… Harrison's language is by turns so punchy, poetic and observant."
- *NY Daily News*

"Mr. Harrison's play has an affectionate, music-loving heart."
- *New York Times*

"Doris to Darlene has much going for it: Harrison's intelligence, originality and passion."
- *Time Out New York*

"Harrison's teasing, rapturous chamber opera of a play spins and crackles like a beloved old 78 under a bamboo needle… *Doris to Darlene* is that rare thing: a rarefied theatrical experiment that has the glow of pure entertainment and the warmth of a folktale."
- *Newsday*

SAMUELFRENCH.COM

EURYDICE
Sarah Ruhl

Dramatic Comedy / 5m, 2f / Unit Set

In *Eurydice*, Sarah Ruhl reimagines the classic myth of Orpheus through the eyes of its heroine. Dying too young on her wedding day, Eurydice must journey to the underworld, where she reunites with her father and struggles to remember her lost love. With contemporary characters, ingenious plot twists, and breathtaking visual effects, the play is a fresh look at a timeless love story.

"RHAPSODICALLY BEAUTIFUL. A weird and wonderful new play - an inexpressibly moving theatrical fable about love, loss and the pleasures and pains of memory."
- The New York Times

"EXHILARATING!! A luminous retelling of the Orpheus myth, lush and limpid as a dream where both author and audience swim in the magical, sometimes menacing, and always thrilling flow of the unconscious."
- *The New Yorker*

"Exquisitely staged by Les Waters and an inventive design team… Ruhl's wild flights of imagination, some deeply affecting passages and beautiful imagery provide transporting pleasures. They conspire to create original, at times breathtaking, stage pictures."
- *Variety*

"Touching, inventive, invigoratingly compact and luminously liquid in its rhythms and design, *Eurydice* reframes the ancient myth of ill-fated love to focus not on the bereaved musician but on his dead bride – and on her struggle with love beyond the grave as both wife and daughter."
- *The San Francisco Chronicle*

SAMUELFRENCH.COM

EVIL DEAD: THE MUSICAL
Book & Lyrics By George Reinblatt
Music By Frank Cipolla/Christopher Bond/Melissa Morris/George Reinblatt

Musical Comedy / 6m, 4f / Unit set

Based on Sam Raimi's 80s cult classic films, *Evil Dead* tells the tale of 5 college kids who travel to a cabin in the woods and accidentally unleash an evil force. And although it may sound like a horror, its not! The songs are hilariously campy and the show is bursting with more farce than a Monty Python skit. *Evil Dead: The Musical* unearths the old familiar story: boy and friends take a weekend getaway at abandoned cabin, boy expects to get lucky, boy unleashes ancient evil spirit, friends turn into Candarian Demons, boy fights until dawn to survive. As musical mayhem descends upon this sleepover in the woods, "camp" takes on a whole new meaning with uproarious numbers like "All the Men in my Life Keep Getting Killed by Candarian Demons," "Look Who's Evil Now" and "Do the Necronomicon."

Outer Critics Circle nomination for
Outstanding New Off-Broadway Musical

"The next Rocky Horror Show!"
- *New York Times*

"A ridiculous amount of fun."
- *Variety*

"Wickedly campy good time."
- *Associated Press*

SAMUELFRENCH.COM